OTSUTOME

Text and Commentary on

Jodo Shu Daily Service

Written and Edited by Taijun KASAHARA

Published by Rinkaian

Jodo Shu Rinkaian
Tama, Tokyo Japan

Taijun KASAHARA
笠原　泰淳
The Chief Priest

Designed by Sougensha, Ltd.

Preface

Taijun KASAHARA

What is Otsutome?

Otsutome is a daily service of about 10 to 30 minutes that Japanese priests and devout believers practice every day in front of the main hall of a temple or Buddhist home altar. *O* is an honorific prefix that expresses respect, and *tsutome* is a word that means practice, service, or work.

While each sect of Buddhism has its own services, Otsutome of Jodo Shu is regarded as being of very high quality. It centers on Nembutsu chanting, chanting sutras, verses, and hymns, aloud.

The Otsutome of Jodo Shu has a very sophisticated structure. I myself have been practicing this service for over 30 years, and from the very beginning I became aware of its profundity.

It consists of three parts: an introductory part, a main part, and an ending part. Centering on the chanting of Nembutsu, it is interspersed with important sentences and verses, and is assembled like one magnificent story.

Moreover, the words of Sakyamuni Buddha and Amida Buddha (Dharmakara Bodhisattva), and the important teachings of Zendo Daishi [善導大師] (Master Shan-tao) and Honen Shonin are included in it. If you know the contents of Otsutome, you will be able to see the overall picture of Jodo Shu, and by extension, the overall picture of Buddhism as seen from Jodo Shu.

For this reason, I have created this textbook in the hope that many people who are interested in Jodo Shu will become familiar with Otsutome.

Like Otsutome, many of the sutras we Japanese usually recite in a temple or at home are based on Chinese translations. Owing to the enormous struggles and efforts by the great masters like Hsuan-tsang [玄奘; 三蔵法師], Buddhist sutras were passed from India to China, where the Indian language was translated into the Chinese language of the time, and then imported into Japan without any modification. Thus, we now recite the sutras in the form of the original Chinese translation.

Therefore, even Japanese cannot understand the meaning of the sutras merely by listening to them. There is a Japanese idiom, "It's just like listening to a sutra," which means "I cannot understand it at all!" rather than "It sounds insightful and profound!"

Thus, although the sutras are hardly comprehensible when you merely listen to them, their meanings are somewhat understandable to those who can read Chinese characters by visually reading their Chinese renderings. The more you study the sutras, the more you will be aware of their hidden charm. I hope English speaking people will experience the pleasure as well.

According to the teachings of Honen Shonin, it is sufficient to simply recite Nembutsu in the practice of the Jodo Shu. Even if you do not recite Otsutome, there is no doubt that Amida Buddha will save you once you have believed in the Original Vow and recited Nembutsu. Retrospectively considered, there was no such service in the time of Honen Shonin.

Nevertheless, as I mentioned before, the content of this service is wonderful, so it helps greatly in the practice of Nembutsu, which tends to be monotonous at times. That's how I've felt for a long time.

In this book, I am trying to make explanations easy to understand for those who do not know Japanese or Chinese so that such explanations are directly connected with actual daily practice. Other English translations of Otsutome are also published by Hawaii Council of Jodo Missions and by Jodo Shu North America Buddhist Missions. However, in this textbook, the translation focuses on the meaning of each *kanji* character rather than an idiomatic translation.

For example, the starting verse of Koge [香偈]:

願我身浄如香炉 gan ga shin jō nyo kō ro,

is explained by seven *kanji* characters having respective meanings as follows:

願 (gan): *wish,*

我 (ga): *my,*

身 (shin): *body,*

浄 (jō): *pure,*

如 (nyo): *like,*

香 (kō): *incense, and*

炉 (ro): *burner,*

and they are interpreted together as:

I wish my body to be pure like an incense burner.

Such a method is applied to all the verses. This is expected to help English-speaking people better understand the original text of the service.

If you think it is too difficult or too long to chant, you don't have to practice the full text from the beginning. I will provide abridged versions at the end of this textbook so that beginners can easily start the practice.

It is said that the prototype of Otsutome was established in the Edo period (*ca.* 16th–17th centuries). Honen Shonin himself seemed to have recited *Amida Sutra* in addition to Nembutsu for a certain period of time, but apparently, he basically recited only Nembutsu. In addition to chanting Nembutsu, the second ancestor Shoko also performed sutra chanting and Raisan (hymns), and these chanting of sutras, Raisan, and Nembutsu became the core of the services of the Jodo Shu thereafter.

Today's Otsutome was developed in the Meiji era (*ca.* 19th century), and consists of the following three parts:

Introductory part:

1 Kōgé (*Incense Verse*),
2 Sanbōraï (*Veneration of the Three Treasures of Buddhism*),
3 Sanbujō (*Welcoming the Buddhas in Three Categories to the Dojo*),
4 Sangégé (*Verse of Repentance*),
5 Jūnen (*Ten recitations of Nembutsu*);

Main part:

6 Raïsan (*Hymn to Amida Buddha and the Pure Land with a melody*),
7 Kaïkyōgé (*Opening Verse for Sutra Chanting*),
8 Shiseigé (*Verse of the Four Vows: an excerpt from Sutra of Immeasurable Life*),
9 Honzeigé (*Verse of the Original Vows*),
10 Jūnen,
11 Ichimaï Kishōmon (*The One-sheet Testament: Honen Shonin's parting message*),
12 Shōyakumon (*Verse of Receiving (Merit of) Salvation: the essential sentence in Meditation Sutra*),

13 Nembutsu Ichié (*A Series of Nembutsu: the central part of the service*),

14 Sōékōgé (*Verse of Merit-transference for All*),

15 Jūnen

Ending part:

16 Sōgangé (*Verse of the Universal Vows of Bodhisattvas*),

17 Sanjinraï (*Bowing to Amida Buddha in Three Virtues*),

18 Sōbutsugé (*Seeing off the Buddhas lastly*),

19 Teisei Jūnen (*Jūnen in a low voice*).

They will be explained one by one in this book.

Description

This sutra text incudes an original text in Chinese characters, their Japanese-style pronunciation in the sutra, and a typical meaning of each character for your information.

The pronunciation is indicated with some accent symbols. For example, 'o' with macron, ō, represents that 'o' is pronounced as a long vowel. The small 'i' with diaeresis, ï, (often following 'a' like 'aï') represents that 'i' is separately pronounced as in "naïve." These are listed below.

ā, ē, ō, ū	Long vowels ([aː], [eː], [oː], [uː]).
ï	Often appearing with preceding 'a' like aï [ai].
é	Often appearing at the end of a word, and pronounced as [e].

Note that the typical meaning of each Chinese character does not always coincide with its meaning in the sutra verses. For example, the word "供養 *ku yō*" is comprised of a character "供" whose original meaning is to serve, offer, etc., and a character "養" meaning to nourish, to make something grow, etc. As a set of the characters, however, it means "offer (to Buddhas)." In such a case, the original meanings are bracketed, and the meaning as the set of characters is put below them.

Sometimes you will find words like "無始 *mu shī*" comprised of a character "無" meaning none, null, or non-, and "始" meaning a beginning or an origin. When they are combined into a set, its meaning becomes "beginningless." This is denoted in this text as "(-less) beginning" following the original arrangement of the characters.

Example

(1) Title of the Verses (with pronunciation)

(2) Meaning of each Chinese character of the title

(3) Pronunciation of the verse

(4) A line of the verse

(5) Typical meanings of each Chinese character

Contents

Appendix

Otsutome

Text and Commentary

Kō gé

香 偈

INCENSE VERSE

Gan	ga	shin	jō	nyo	kō	ro
願	我	身	浄	如	香	炉
WISH	*MY*	*BODY*	*PURE*	*LIKE*	*INCENSE*	*BURNER*

Gan	ga	shin	nyo	chi	é	ka
願	我	心	如	智	慧	火
WISH	*MY*	*HEART*	*LIKE*	*INTELLECT WISDOM*	*BRILLIANCE*	*FIRE*

Nen	nen	bon	jō	kaï	jō	kō
念	念	焚	燒	戒	定	香
MINDFUL	*THOUGHT*	*KINDLE*	*BURN*	*SILA*	*SAMADHI*	*INCENSE*

Ku	yō	ji	ppō	san	zé	bu
供	養	十	方	三	世	仏
[SERVE OFFER	*NOURISH]*	*TEN*	*DIRECTION*	*THREE*	*PERIOD*	*BUDDHA*

Incense Verse

{ *Burning incense to purify our body and mind* }

I wish my body to be pure like an incense burner.

I wish my heart to be like a lamp of wisdom.

With mindful thought, I burn the incense of sila and samadhi[1].

To offer the lamp and incense[2] to the buddhas of the ten directions[3] (i.e., in all directions) in the three periods (i.e., past, present, and future.)

---

[1] *Sila* is the moral internal standards in Buddhism, and *samadhi* is meditation. This phrase means, "By mindfully burning incense, I wish to create a similar religious atmosphere that could be got from the practice of *sila* and *samadhi*."

[2] The metaphor of merits of the practice of *sila*, *samadhi*, and wisdom.

[3] Eight horizontal directions (N, S, E W, NE, NW, SE, and SW) and two vertical directions (upward and downward).

Koge is a verse from *Hojisan* [法事讃] by Zendo Daishi.

At the beginning of Otsutome, we burn incense to purify our body and mind, and declare that we will offer a service to the Buddhas.

Incense has been traditionally used for several purposes. It is used for removing offensive odors, for repelling insects, for calming the mind, for attracting the opposite sex, and the like. In Buddhism, incense is mainly used to clean or purify one's body and mind, and to venerate buddhas. Incense that is spread over one's body is called *Zuko* ([塗香]; finely powdered incense for application), and incense that is burned is called *Shoko* ([焼香]; granulated incense for burning). Incense sticks ([線香] *Senko*), which are widely known and probably most easily available, are one kind of *Shoko*.

Burning incense of good quality and suited to your taste indeed makes your mind calm and relaxed. If someone asks me to give a succinct outline of Buddhist teachings, I would answer "Buddhist teachings aim to keep your mind calm and to help you live your life honestly and fairly." What is meant by keeping one's mind calm is not only to retreat alone avoiding troubles, though sometimes it is required. Rather, I would like to say that to address various problems in one's life, it is very important to keep one's mind calm. Contemplating one's inner self or others with a serene mind, exchanging sincere smiles from deep within our hearts, and sharing one's sadness with tears… these will spontaneously soothe away any anger or covetousness.

Observance of precepts and meditation are fundamental to Buddhist practice. Judging from the teachings of Jodo Shu, some may wonder whether there is no need to follow the precepts or meditate. Here, it would be fine if you chant Koge with the feeling that you have cultivated these things and purify your body and mind.

Upon starting Otsutome, burn the tip of one stick of Senko, for example, and set it upright in the center of ash filled in a burner (or set it in an incense holder). Alternatively, apply a pinch of Zuko and spread it over your hands. Then, smell the aroma, and let's start Otsutome.

You can start Otsutome with the simplest alter like this.

San bō raï

三 宝 礼

THREE   TREASURE   BOW

I-　　sshin　kyō　raï

一　　心　　敬　　礼

[ONE   HEART]   RESPECT   BOW
WHOLEHEARTEDLY

ji-　　ppō　hō　kaï　jō　jū　bu

十　　方　　法　　界　　常　　住　　仏

TEN   DIRECTION DHARMA   REALM   ETERNAL   EXIST   BUDDHA

I-　　sshin　kyō　raï

一　　心　　敬　　礼

ji-　　ppō　hō　kaï　jō　jū　hō

十　　方　　法　　界　　常　　住　　法

DHARMA

I-　　sshin　kyō　raï

一　　心　　敬　　礼

ji-　　ppō　hō　kaï　jō　jū　sō

十　　方　　法　　界　　常　　住　　僧

SANGHA

Veneration of the Three Treasures

Worshiping the Three Treasures as a Buddhist

I wholeheartedly and respectfully bow down to
(i.e., take refuge in)

the Buddhas who eternally exist
in the Dharma Realms of the ten directions.

I wholeheartedly and respectfully bow down to
(i.e., take refuge in)

the Dharma that eternally exists
in the Dharma Realms of the ten directions.

I wholeheartedly and respectfully bow down to
(i.e., take refuge in)

the Sanghas that eternally exist
in the Dharma Realms of the ten directions.

Sanborai is a verse from *Ojo Jodo Sangangi* [往生浄土懺願儀] (Repentance Rituals for Birth in the Pure Land) by Ven. Jiun Sonja ([慈雲尊者], or Junshiki [遵式]).

There are three treasures that Buddhism holds dear. They are Buddha, Dharma, *i.e.*, Buddha's teachings, and Sangha, *i.e.*, a community of monks and nuns. In the time of Sakyamuni Buddha, Sangha meant a gathering of ordained monks and nuns who worshiped Sakyamuni. However, since Jodo Shu is descended from Mahayana Buddhism, especially in this Nembutsu teaching, both monks and lay believers are equally saved through Nembutsu. Therefore, when we say "Sangha," we imply a gathering of Buddhists, including ordinary believers.

It is only in the presence of Buddha, teachings told by Him, and people who listened to His teachings that Buddhism is able to be preached. Buddhism as a religion could not exist without any one of the three treasures. We respect these three treasures wholeheartedly and bow our head deeply—this is Sanborai.

The phrase "Buddhas, Dharma, and Sanghas that eternally exist in the dharma realms of the ten directions" needs to be more particularly explained.

Sometime after Sakyamuni passed away, a compelling question arose: "Who guides us after Sakyamuni's death?" The question led to the introduction of many Buddhas and Buddha-lands into preaching. This is one of major characteristics of Mahayana Buddhism. While taking refuge in the three treasures has been practiced as an initiation to Buddhism since the time of Sakyamuni Buddha, the teaching of "Buddhas, Dharma, and Sanghas that **eternally exist in the dharma realms of the ten directions**" is specific to Mahayana Buddhism. The same applies to the last line of Koge, "the buddhas of the ten directions in the three periods."

Note)   In Jodo Shu, there has been an idea that Buddha, Dharma and Sangha are equivalent, respectively, to Amida Buddha, the three Pure Land Sutras, and holy people of the Pure Land. Here, however, Sanborai is interpreted as a general devotion to the three treasures without going that far.

San bu jō

三　奉　請

THREE　REVERENTLY　INVOKE

Bu-	jō	mi	da	sé	son
奉	請	弥	陀	世	尊
[REVER-ENTLY WELCOMING	*INVOKE]*	*(A)MI-*	*DA*	*WORLD*	*HONORED*

		nyū	dō	jō
		入	道	場
		ENTER	*PRACTICE*	*PLACE*

Bu-	jō	sha	ka	nyo	raï
奉	請	釈	迦	如	来
		SA-	*KYA*	*[THUS TATHAGATA*	*COME]*

		nyū	dō	jō
		入	道	場

Bu-	jō	ji-	ppō	nyo	raï
奉	請	十	方	如	来
		TEN	*DIRECTION*	*TATHAGATA*	

		nyū	dō	jō
		入	道	場

Welcoming Buddhas in Three Categories

❧ Welcoming the Buddhas to the dojo ❧

We reverently pray to Amida Buddha, the World Honored One,

that He may enter this practice place.

We reverently pray to Sakyamuni Tathagata

that He may enter this practice place.

We reverently pray to Tathagatas of the ten directions

that They may enter this practice place.

Sanbujo is a verse from *Hojisan* [法事讃] (Praise of Dharma Services) by Zendo Daishi, as with Koge.

Now that we have purified our body and mind with Koge, and expressed our devotion to the Three Treasures to prepare our hearts, we then welcome the Buddhas who will lead and save us.

In Jodo Shu, there are three categories of Buddhas.

First, Amida Buddha is the object of devotion who leads us to His Pure Land.

Secondly, Sakyamuni Buddha or Sakyamuni Tathagata is the One who taught us the Pure Land Way.

Lastly, there are other Buddhas or Tathagatas who attest the genuineness of the Pure Land Way. The attesting constitutes part of the most important teachings preached in *Amida Sutra*.

Chanting Sanbujo, we welcome all these Buddhas in this dojo (practice place).

3

San gé gé

懺 悔 偈

REPENT VERSE

Ga	shaku	sho	zō	sho	aku	gō
我	昔	所	造	諸	悪	業
I	*PAST*	*(WHAT)*	*CREATE*	*VARIOUS*	*EVIL*	*KARMA*

Kaï	yu	mu	shi	ton	jin	chi
皆	由	無	始	貪	瞋	痴
ALL	*BECAUSE*	*(-LESS)*	*BEGINNING*	*GREED*	*ANGER*	*DELUSION*

Jū	shin	go	ï	shi	sho	shō
從	身	語	意	之	所	生
FROM	*BODY*	*WORD*	*MIND*	*(OF)*	*(WHICH)*	*BORN*

I-	ssaï	ga	kon	kaï	san	gé
一	切	我	今	皆	懺	悔
[ONE	*WHOLE]*	*I*	*NOW*	*ALL*	*[REPENT*	*REGRET]*
EVERY (KARMA)					*REPENT*	

Verse of Repentance

Repenting our evil karmas before the Buddhas

The various evil karmas that I have created in the past

Were all caused by my greed, anger and delusion
since the beginning-less time,

And born of my body (physical acts), words, and mind (thoughts).

I now repent the whole of them.

Sangege is a verse from the "Praises of the Practices and Vows of Samantabhadra Bodhisattva" [普賢菩薩行願品] in the "Forty-volume *Kegon-kyo*" [四十巻本華厳経] (*Avataṃsaka Sutra*—The Flower Garland Sutra).

In Jodo Shu, Sange [懺悔], repentance, is very important. Only after we know our evil karmas and repent them, can we really know that the Power of the Vow of Amida would be our single hope.

We are here now as a result of transmigration, an endless circle of birth and death in a world of delusion. Because of the fact that we are now in the circle of transmigration, we inevitably have to admit that we have never attained enlightenment before.

This ignorant self has been bound by worldly desires represented by the three poisons. The three poisons are insatiable desire (greed), anger, and narrow-minded ignorance (delusion). These poisons have kept us from enlightenment, and have produced our evil deeds (evil karma).

These evil deeds have been embodied through the three channels of body (physical actions), words (lying, exaggerating, etc.), and mind (holding evil thought). "Now I repent of all of these in front of the Buddhas whom I have welcomed here today. I then declare that in the future, I will try to stop the evil deeds."

Awareness of this evil karma deepens our faith in Amida Buddha, the only Being who can save us from transmigration. (This subject will be also addressed in the explanation of the Three Minds (Sanjin [三心]) in *Ichimai Kishomon*.)

4

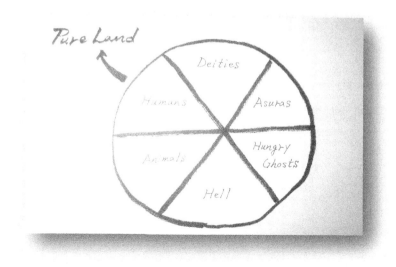

Jū　nen

十　　念

TEN　　NEMBUTSU

Na mu a mi da bu　　Na mu a mi da bu
南無阿弥陀仏　　南無阿弥陀仏

Na mu a mi da bu　　Na mu a mi da bu
南無阿弥陀仏　　南無阿弥陀仏

Na mu a mi da bu　　Na mu a mi da bu
南無阿弥陀仏　　南無阿弥陀仏

Na mu a mi da bu　　Na mu a mi da bu
南無阿弥陀仏　　南無阿弥陀仏

Na mu a mi da butsu Na- mu a mi da bu-
南無阿弥陀仏　　南無阿弥陀仏

Ten recitations of Nembutsu

In the word Junen, *ju* means "ten," and *nen* means "reciting Nembutsu" here, so that Junen is interpreted as ten recitations of Nembutsu.

Junen is preached in the 18th Original Vow of Dharmakara Bodhisattva in *Sutra of Immeasurable Life* [無量寿経] (*Mu ryo ju kyo*).

When I attain Buddhahood,
if all sentient beings of the ten directions,
who aspire in all sincerity and faith to be born in my land and call my name
even ten times, are not born there,
then may I not attain supreme enlightenment.
Excluded, however, are those who commit the five gravest offences and
abuse the right Dharma.

(*Sutra of Immeasurable Life*)

Since the *kanji* "念" usually means *thinking of* or *remembering*, the phrase "call my name even ten times" [乃至十念] (*nai shi ju nen*) originally means "thinking of Amida Buddha even ten times."

Based on the teaching of Zendo Daishi, Honen Shonin advocated that the word *nen* [念] is the same as vocalization [声], or recitation, and the idea is expressed as "念声是一" (*nen sho ze itsu*, in which "是一" means "the same") in Senchakushu (*cf.* Chapter 3).

In Jodo Shu, therefore, Junen means ten recitations of Nembutsu, that is, Amida Buddha's name, and is the most basic and essential practice of Jodo Shu.

In practice, after the eighth recitation of "Namu Amidabu," breathe in, and then say, "Namu Amidabu**tsu**, Namu Amidabu." We say the last Namu Amidabu while making a bow to Amida. (When chanting the first eight recitations of Nembutsu, a breath may be taken after chanting four times.)

The *kanji* characters 南無阿弥陀仏 are phonetic notation of "na mu a mi da butsu," in which *namu* means that I will take refuge in You, and that I will entrust You with my salvation; *amida butsu* is the name as a buddha of Dharmakara Bodhisattva after he attained perfect enlightenment. *A* is a prefix

19

indicating negation, and *mida* means to measure, which is similar to the English word meter. Butsu means a buddha.

Therefore, the original meaning of Namu Amida Butsu is that I entrust my salvation to Amida Buddha, the immeasurable Buddha.

Specifically, the immeasurable Buddha, as it is said in *Amida Sutra*, means that the light radiated by the Buddha is infinite, and that the lifespan of the Buddha is immeasurable.

The response to "Call my name" in the 18th Vow is "Yes, I will call your name. Please save me into the Pure Land," which means to chant "Namu Amida Bu(tsu)."

This chanting is called Nembutsu.

Jodo Shu priests often call out to participants, "同称十念—*Dō shō jū nen*." *Dō* [同] is an adverb meaning "together," and *shō* [称] means "recite." Thus, by saying "同称十念," they say, "Let's chant ten recitations of Nembutsu together."

5

礼　讃

BOW　　PRAISE

Nā[4]	mū	shī	shi in	kī	myō ō	rāï
南	無	至	心	帰	命	礼
NA-	MU	[ULTIMATE	HEART]	[RETURN	DECREE]	BOW
		WHOLEHEARTEDLY		TAKE REFUGE IN		

Sa aï	hō	A	mi	dā	Bū
西	方	阿	弥	陀	仏
WEST	DIRECTION	A-	MI-	DA	BUDDHA

Mī	dā	shin	jiki	nyō	kon	sē en
弥	陀	身	色	如	金	山
(A)MI-	DA	BODY	FORM	LIKE	GOLD	MOUNTAIN

Sō	gō	kō	myō	shō	ji-	ppo o
相	好	光	明	照	十	方
[MARK	PREFERABLE]	LIGHT	BRIGHT-	ILLUMINATE	TEN	DIRECTION
APPEARANCE			NESS			

Yuï	ū	nen	butsu	mū	kō	sho o
唯	有	念	仏	蒙	光	摂
SOLELY	PRESENT	[THOUGHT	BUDDHA]	RECEIVE	LIGHT	SAVE
		NEMBUTSU (RECITERS)				

To o	chī	hon	gan	sa aï	ī	go o
当	知	本	願	最	為	強
JUST	KNOW	ORIGINAL	VOW	MOST	BE	POWERFUL

---

[4] Pronunciation is denoted according to the melody.

Hymn of Praise to Amida and the Pure Land

❧ Praising Amida Buddha and the Pure Land with a melody ❧

I wholeheartedly take refuge in and bow down

To Amida Buddha in the western direction.

The form of Amida's body appears like a golden mountain.

The light emanating from the (appearance of the) body
illuminates in the ten directions.

Solely the Nembutsu reciters receive the light of salvation.

Just know that the Original Vow is the most powerful.

| Ro-
六
SIX | ppō
方
DIRECTION | nyō
如
[THUS | ra aï
来
COME]
TATHAGATA | jō
舒
EXTEND | ze-
舌
TONGUE | sho o
証
CERTIFY |

| Sen
専
EXCLUSIVELY | shō
称
CHANT | myō
名
[NAME | gō
号
DESIGNATION]
NAME OF AMIDA | shī
至
REACH | sa aï
西
WEST | ho o
方
DIRECTION |

| Tō
到
REACH | hī
彼
THERE | kē
華
FLOWER | kaï
開
OPEN | mon
聞
LISTEN | myō
妙
GRACEFUL | ho o
法
DHARMA |

| Ju u
十
TEN | jī
地
STAGE | gan
願
VOW | gyō
行
PRACTICE | ji i
自
[SELF | nen
然
MANNER]
NATURALLY | jo o
彰
REVEAL |

| Gan
願
WISH | gū
共
TOGETHER | shō
諸
VARIOUS | shū
衆
[PEOPLE | jō
生
LIFE]
SENTIENT BEINGS |

| Ō
往
[GO
BE BORN | jō
生
BORN] | an
安
SERENE | ra a-
楽
PEACEFUL | kkōkū
国
LAND |

The tathagatas (buddhas) of the six directions
have extended their tongues to certify

That those who exclusively chant the name of Amida
can reach the Pure Land in the west.

Reaching there (the Pure Land), our lotus flower will open and we can listen to the 妙 *(graceful, marvelous, wondrous) dharma (that Amida preaches).*

Then the ten stages of the vows and practices
(as a bodhisattva) will naturally reveal themselves clearly.

We wish, together with various sentient beings (many people[5]),

To go and be born in the serene and peaceful (blissful) Land
(of Amida).

---

[5] While what the term 'sentient beings' refers to or includes can be contemplated in several ways, I interpret it mainly as "people" here because only human beings are capable of wishing to be born in the Pure Land and practicing Nembutsu.

Nā	mū	shī	shi	in	kī	myo o	rāī
南	無	至	心	帰	命	礼

Sa aï	hō	A	mi	dā	Bū
西	方	阿	弥	陀	仏

Aï	min	fū	go o	ga ā
哀	愍	覆	護	我
SYMPATHY	COMPASSION	COVER	PROTECT	ME

Ryo o	bō	shū	zō	jo o
令	法	種	増	長
(MAKE)	DHARMA	SEED	INCREASE	GROW

Shī	sē	gyū	gō	sho o
此	世	及	後	生
THIS	WORLD	AND	FUTURE	LIFE

Gan	butsu	jō	shō	ju u
願	仏	常	摂	受
WISH	BUDDHA	CONSTANT	SAVE	RECEIVE

Gan	gū	sho o	shu ū	jō
願	共	諸	衆	生

Ō	jo o	an	rā-	kkōkū
往	生	安	楽	国

I wholeheartedly take refuge in and bow down

To Amida Buddha in the western direction.

May Buddha envelop and protect me
                              with Your sympathy and compassion.

(And may Buddha) make the dharma seed (in my mind)
increase (in size) and grow.

In this world (life) and in the future life,

I wish Buddha to save and receive (me) constantly.

We wish, together with various sentient beings (many people),

To go and be born in the serene and peaceful (blissful) Land
                                          (of Amida).

Raisan（礼讃）

Na mu shi shi in ki myo o rai Sa ai ho A mi da Bu

Ai min fu go-o ga a Ryo-o bo shu zo jo o

Shi se gyu go sho - o Gam bu tsu jo sho ju – u

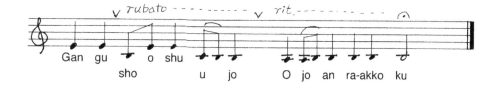

Gan gu o shu sho u jo O jo an ra-akko ku

Raisan is a short selection from *Rokuji Raisan* [六時礼讃] (Praise of Amida Buddha and the Pure Land Six Times a Day), written by Zendo Daishi.

It is chanted in the *shomyo* [声明] style (*i.e.*, with a melody).

The following is a phrase-by-phrase explanation.

南無至心帰命礼 (p. 22, l. 1)

I wholeheartedly take refuge in and bow down...

南無 (namu):   taking refuge in, and

至心 (shishin): 至 (shi) means to be ultimate and 心 (shin) means "mind" or "heart." The Chinese character 心 is a pictograph of heart. Thus, *Shishin* means "the ultimate mind/heart that is directed towards Amida Buddha in the Pure Land." Shishin also means sincerity in general.

帰命 (kimyo):   the same meaning as Namu.

    帰: returning/going to the ultimate destination

    命: decree/life/destiny

礼 (rai): bowing down

弥陀身色如金山/相好光明照十方/唯有念仏蒙光摂 (p. 22, ll. 3–5)

The form of Amida's body appears like a golden mountain.
The light emanating from the (appearance of the) body
illuminates in the ten directions.
Solely the Nembutsu reciters receive the light of salvation.

From "Mida shinjiki nyo konsen" to "Yui u Nembutsu mu kosho" corresponds to the content of the ninth visualization of *Meditation Sutra*, as in Shoyakumon.

当知本願最為強 (p. 22, l. 6)

Just know that the Original Vow is the most powerful.

This refers to the saving power of the 18th Vow of Amida Buddha (Dharmakara Bodhisattva), which was touched on in the "Junen" section.

六方如来舒舌証/専称名号至西方 (p. 24, ll. 1–2)

The tathagatas (buddhas) of the six directions have extended their tongues to certify
That those who exclusively chant the name of Amida can reach the Pure Land in the west.

In *Amida Sutra*, Sakyamuni Buddha preaches that the buddhas of the six directions, as countless as the sands of Ganges, extended their tongues throughout the three-thousand-great-thousand worlds and proclaimed that the teaching of Birth in the Pure Land through Nembutsu is true. Please refer to the explanation of "十方如来 (*jippo nyorai*)" in Sanbujo. Extending the tongue symbolizes telling the truth in ancient India.

到彼華開聞妙法 (p. 24, l. 3)

Reaching there (the Pure Land), our lotus flower will open and we can listen to the 妙 (graceful, marvelous, wondrous) dharma (that Amida preaches).

We will be born in a lotus bud in the Pure Land after our death. Then, the bud will bloom.

十地願行自然彰 (p. 24, l. 4)

Then the ten stages of the vows and practices (as a bodhisattva) will naturally reveal themselves clearly.

十地 (jūji):   The ten stages of developing the Buddha-wisdom.

According to a dictionary of Buddhist terms[6], the ten stages are:
1)   joy at benefitting oneself and others;
2)   freedom from all possible defilement;
3)   emission of the light of wisdom;
4)   glowing wisdom;
5)   overcoming utmost difficulties;
6)   realization of wisdom;

---

[6] Japanese-English Buddhist Dictionary [Revised Edition] (Published by Daito Publishing Co., Inc., 1991) See also https://www.daitopb.co.jp/5819.html.

7) proceeding far;

8) attainment of immobility;

9) attainment of expedient wisdom; and

10) ability to spread the teachings over the dharma-dhatu as clouds overspread the sky.

This is the answer to what will happen after your Birth in the Pure Land. Your lotus flower will open, you can directly meet Amida Buddha and the bodhisattvas, and attain the high ten stages toward Buddhahood.

願共諸衆生/往生安楽国 (p. 24, ll. 5–6)

They are repeated one more time later. See below.

哀愍覆護我/令法種増長/此世及後生/願仏常摂受 (p. 26, ll. 3–6)

May Buddha envelop and protect me with Your sympathy and compassion.
(And may Buddha) make the dharma seed (in my mind) increase (in size)
and grow.
In this world (life) and in the future life,
I wish Buddha to save and receive (me) constantly.

Zendo Daishi

These four lines are found in *Śrīmālādevī-siṃhanāda-sūtra* [勝鬘経] (The Lion's Roar of Queen Srimala Sutra). It is found in several places in *Rokuji Raisan* and is used as a verse to pray for the protection of Buddha.

願共諸衆生/往生安楽国 (p. 26, ll. 7–8)

We wish, together with various sentient beings (many people[7]),
To go and be born in the serene and peaceful (blissful) Land (of Amida).

Repeated the second time. These two lines also appear many times in *Rokuji Raisan*. I believe this wish is the very thing Zendo Daishi wanted to tell us the most.

---

[7] While what the term 'sentient beings' refers to or includes can be contemplated in several ways, I interpret it mainly as "people" here because only human beings are capable of wishing to be born in the Pure Land and practicing Nembutsu.

Kaï kyō gé

開 経 偈

OPEN   SUTRA   VERSE

Mu	jō	jin	jin	mi	myō	hō
無	上	甚	深	微	妙	法
UN-	*SURPASSED*	*VERY*	*DEEP*	*DELICATE*	*GRACEFUL*	*DHARMA*

Hyaku	sen	man	gō	nan	sō	gū
百	千	万	劫	難	遭	遇
HUNDRED	*THOUSAND*	*TEN-THOUSAND*	*KALPA*	*DIFFICULT*	*ENCOUNTER*	*MEET*

Ga	kon	ken	mon	toku	ju	ji
我	今	見	聞	得	受	持
I	*NOW*	*LOOK*	*LISTEN*	*GAIN*	*RECEIVE*	*RETAIN*

Gan	gé	nyo	raï	shin	jitsu	gi
願	解	如	来	真	実	義
WISH	*UNDERSTAND*	*[THUS*	*COME]*	*[TRUE*	*SUBSTANTIAL]*	*PATH*
		TATHAGATA		*GENUINE*		

Opening Verse for Sutra Chanting

The unsurpassed, very deep (profound), delicate, and
                              graceful dharma (teachings),

Even after a hundred, thousand, million kalpa (eons), is
                              difficult to encounter (meet).

I have now looked at it, listened to it, and received and retained it.

I wish to understand the true message of the Tathagata (Buddha).

7

As mentioned earlier, Otsutome consists of three parts, an introductory part, a main part, and the last, ending part. From this Kaikyoge, we proceed to the second, main part. (Raisan should be originally included in this main part, but it is also allowed to chant before Kaikyoge as an exception.)

Kaikyoge is the opening verse for sutra chanting. The source of this verse is unknown. The verse is recited not only by Jodo Shu but also by other Buddhist sects. That is, following Kaikyoge, the sutras on which each sect is based are chanted.

Bussetsu Mu ryō ju kyō

仏説無量寿経

BUDDHA PREACH (-LESS) MEASURE LIFETIME SUTRA

Shi sei gé

四誓偈

FOUR VOW VERSE

Ga gon chō se gan

我建超世願

I ESTABLISH [SUPER WORLD] VOW
SURPASSING

Hi- sshi mu jō dō

必至無上道

SURELY REACH UN- SURPASSED PATH

Shi gan fu man zoku

斯願不満足

THIS VOW NOT MEET FILL

Sei fu jō shō gaku

誓不成正覚

VOW NOT ATTAIN RIGHT ENLIGHTENMENT

Ga o mu ryō kō

我於無量劫

I OVER (-LESS) MEASURE KALPA

Fu i daï sé shu

不為大施主

NOT BECOME GREAT [BENEFIT MASTER]
BENEFACTOR

Verse of the FOUR VOWS in the Sutra of Immeasurable Life preached by Buddha

§ *Excerpt from Sutra of Immeasurable Life* §

I[8] have established the (forty-eight) vows
which are beyond the world.

I will surely reach the unsurpassed path
(by fulfilling the vows).

If the vows are not fulfilled,

I vow not to attain the perfect enlightenment
(as I expressed in each vow).

(In conclusion, He, Dharmakara Bodhisattva, attained the perfect
enlightenment later on, and reached the unsurpassed path (to save
all sentient beings).)

Should I, in measureless kalpa (eons),

not become a great benefactor

---

[8] Dharmakara Bodhisattva himself. See the explanation below.

Fu	saï	sho	bin	gu
普	済	諸	貧	苦
WIDELY	RELIEVE	VARIOUS	POVERTY	AGONY

Sei	fu	jō	shō	gaku
誓	不	成	正	覚
VOW	NOT	ATTAIN	RIGHT	ENLIGHTENMENT

Ga	shi	jō	butsu	dō
我	至	成	仏	道
I	REACH	ATTAIN	BUDDHA	PATH

Myō	shō	chō	ji-	ppō
名	声	超	十	方
NAME	SOUND	REACH	TEN	DIRECTION

Ku	kyō	mi	sho	mon
究	竟	靡	所	聞
ATTAIN	ULTIMACY	NOT	(BE)	HEARD

Sei	fu	jō	shō	gaku
誓	不	成	正	覚
VOW	NOT	ATTAIN	RIGHT	ENLIGHTENMENT

Ri	yoku	jin	shō	nen
離	欲	深	正	念
AVOID	DESIRE	DEEP	RIGHT	MINDFULNESS

Jō	é	shu	bon	gyō
浄	慧	修	梵	行
PURE	WISDOM	PRACTICE	[CHASTITY	PRACTICE]
				CELIBACY

And widely relieve those who in various poverty and agony,

I vow not to attain the perfect enlightenment.

When I reach the attainment of the path of Buddha,

my name shall resound and reach the worlds of ten directions.

Should there be any place in which it cannot be heard,

I vow not to attain the perfect enlightenment.

(In conclusion, He, Dharmakara Bodhisattva, attained the perfect enlightenment later on, and after that, He has been saving and will save all beings everywhere through His Name.)

Through the avoiding desire, profound right mindfulness,

pure wisdom, and practicing celibacy,

Shi	gu	mu	jō	dō
志	求	無	上	道
ASPIRE	SEEK	UN-	SURPASSED	PATH

	I	sho	ten	nin	shi
	為	諸	天	人	師
	BECOME	VARIOUS	CELESTIAL	MORTAL	TEACHER

Jin	riki	en	daï	kō
神	力	演	大	光
SUPERNATURAL	POWER	DEVELOP	GREAT	LIGHT

	Fu	shō	mu	saï	do
	普	照	無	際	土
	UNIVERSALLY ILLUMINATE		(-LESS)	BOUNDARY	LAND

Shō	jo	san	ku	myō
消	除	三	垢	冥
ERASE	REMOVE	THREE	GRIME	DARKNESS

	Kō	saï	shū	yaku	nan
	広	済	衆	厄	難
	BROADLY	RELIEVE	PEOPLE	CALAMITY	DIFFICULTY

Kaï	hi	chi	é	gen
開	彼	智	慧	眼
OPEN	THAT	[INTELLECT BRILLIANT] WISDOM		EYE

	Me-	sshi	kon	mō	an
	滅	此	昏	盲	闇
	ELIMINATE	THIS	OBSCURE	BLIND	DARKNESS

I shall aspire and seek the unsurpassed (ultimate) path

> *to become a teacher of various celestials and mortals.*

[Like Lokesvararaja Buddha, a buddha's] divine power develops and produces a great light,

> *which light universally illuminates boundless lands,*

And erases and removes the darkness of the three defilements (greed, anger, and delusion)

> *to broadly relieve people from calamities and difficulties.*

(Dharmakara praises the high virtue of Lokesvararaja and other buddhas.)

[Like You, Lokesvararaja Buddha, a buddha] opens their (the people's) eye of wisdom,

> *eliminates their sunset-like, blind darkness,*

43

Hei	soku	sho	aku	dō
閉	塞	諸	悪	道
CLOSE	BLOCK	VARIOUS	EVIL	PATH

Tsū	datsu	zen	ju	mon
通	達	善	趣	門
PASS	ATTAIN	[GOOD DISPOSITION] GOOD WORLD		GATE

Ku	so	jō	man	zoku
功	祚	成	満	足
[MERIT HIGHNESS] VIRTUE		ATTAIN	MEET	FILL

I	yō	rō	ji-	ppō
威	曜	朗	十	方
PRESTIGE	GLOW	BRIGHT	TEN	DIRECTION

Nichi	ga-	sshū	jū	ki
日	月	戢	重	暉
SUN	MOON	WEAKEN	COMPLEX	LUMINANCE

Ten	kō	on	pu	gen
天	光	隠	不	現
CELESTIAL	LIGHT	HIDE	NOT	APPEAR

I	shū	kaï	hō	zō
為	衆	開	法	蔵
FOR	PEOPLE	OPEN	DHARMA	REPOSITORY

Kō	sé	ku	doku	hō
広	施	功	徳	宝
BROADLY	GIVE	[MERIT VIRTUE]	VIRTUE	TREASURE

Closes and blocks the various evil paths
(of hells, hungry ghosts, and animals)

to make them pass and attain the gate of the good
worlds (i.e., the worlds of gods and human)

Fulfilling the high virtues,

a buddha extends the majestic radiance to the ten
directions.

The overlapped light of the sun and moon is outshone
(in the radiance), and

the lights of heavens are also hidden and don't
appear.

For the sake of people, a buddha opens the repository of the
dharma and

broadly gives the meritorious and virtuous treasure.

Jō	o	daï	shū	jū
常	於	大	衆	中
CONSTANTLY	AT	GREAT	PEOPLE	AMONG

Sé-	ppō	shi	shi	ku
説	法	獅	子	吼
PREACH	DHARMA	[LION	ANIMAL]	ROAR
			LION	

Ku	yō	i-	ssaï	butsu
供	養	一	切	仏
[SERVE	NOURISH]	[ONE	WHOLE]	BUDDHA
OFFER			ALL	

Gu	soku	shū	toku	hon
具	足	衆	徳	本
ENDOWED	FILL	MANY	VIRTUE	ROOT

Gan	né	shitsu	jō	man
願	慧	悉	成	満
VOW	WISDOM	TOTALLY	ATTAIN	MEET

Toku	i	san	gaï	o
得	為	三	界	雄
GAIN	BECOME	THREE	REALM	HERO

Nyo	butsu	mu	gé	chi
如	仏	無	礙	智
LIKE	BUDDHA	(-LESS)	HINDRANCE	WISDOM

Tsū	datsu	mi	fu	shō
通	達	靡	不	照
PASS	ATTAIN	NOT	NOT	ILLUMINATE

And among a great number of people,

He preaches the dharma constantly with a lion's roar.

Making offerings to all the buddhas,

becoming endowed with many roots of virtue,

Fulfilling the vows and attaining wisdom totally,

a buddha becomes a hero of the Three Realms[9]
(of the unenlightened beings).

A buddha's unimpeded wisdom reaches all,

leaving nowhere not illuminated.

---

[9] The realm of attachment to sensuous desire, the realm of attachment to form, and the realm of attachment to formlessness. See Glossary.

Gan	ga	ku	é	riki
願	我	功	慧	力
VOW	MY	VIRTUE	WISDOM	POWER

	Tō	shi	saï	shō	son
	等	此	最	勝	尊
	EQUAL	THIS	MOST	SUPERIOR	ONE

Shi	gan	nya-	kko-	kka
斯	願	若	剋	果
THIS	VOW	IF	ACCOMPLISH	FINISH

	Daï	sen	ō	kan	dō
	大	千	応	感	動
	[GREAT THOUSAND] UNIVERSE		RESPONSE	[IMPRESS SENSATION	MOVE]

Ko	kū	sho	ten	nin
虚	空	諸	天	人
EMPTY	SKY	VARIOUS	CELESTIAL	BEING

	Tō	u	chin	myō	ké
	当	雨	珍	妙	華
	SURELY	RAIN	RARE	GRACEFUL	FLOWER

I vow that the power of my virtue and wisdom

will be equal to the Most Superior Venerable One.

If these vows are fulfilled,

the whole universe will tremble in response.

Various celestial beings in the sky

will rain down rare and graceful flowers.

8

This is a story in the *Sutra of Immeasurable Life* preached by Sakyamuni Buddha.

Long, long ago, there was a practitioner named Dharmakara Bodhisattva ([法 蔵菩薩], *Hozo Bosatsu*) who made 48 vows in order to build an ideal Buddha land in front of his master, Lokeshvararaja Buddha ([世自在王仏], *Se-jizai-ou Butsu*). After making the vows, Dharmakara Bodhisattva himself summarized these 48 vows in four. This is Shiseige.

Among the 48 vows are the vows to make this Buddha land a world without suffering from the three evil paths, and to ensure that those who are born in this Buddha land can attain Buddhahood. The most important vow is the 18th Vow of Nembutsu Ojo. (Explained in **5** Junen)

These vows are called Original Vows in the sense that they were vows made when Amida Buddha was still a bodhisattva. Later, Dharmakara Bodhisattva fulfilled these vows and became Amida Buddha. At that point, these vows became promises that Amitabha Buddha would surely fulfill.

In Jodo Shu, it is customary to recite a passage from the three Pure Land Sutras following **9** Kaikyoge. Shiseige is extremely important passage preached as a summary of the Original Vows, which is the origin of Hongan Nembutsu, so it is recited most frequently in Jodo Shu.

The four vows in Shiseige are:

1) to reach the ultimate path of enlightenment (the fulfilment of the 48 vows) (p. 38, ll. 1–4);

2) to guide all from poverty and suffering (p. 38, ll. 5–6 and p. 40, ll. 1–2);

3) to save all beings everywhere through His Name (p. 40, ll. 3–6); and

4) to become equal to Lokeshvararaja Buddha in regard to the power of the virtue and wisdom, and if these vows are to be realized, some miracles will appear (p. 48, ll. 5–6 and p. 48, ll. 1–4).

8

Hon zei gé

本 誓 偈

ORIGINAL *VOW* *VERSE*

Mi　　　da　　　hon　　　zei　　　gan

弥　　　陀　　　本　　　誓　　　願

(A)MI-　　*DA*　　*ORIGINAL*　　*VOW*　　*WISH*

Goku　　raku　　shi　　yō　　mon

極　　楽　　之　　要　　門

[ULTIMATE　　*BLISS]*　　*'S*　　*PRINCIPAL*　　*GATE*

SUKHAVATI

Jō　　san　　tō　　é　　kō

定　　散　　等　　回　　向

CONCENTRA-　*DISTRACTION*　*EQUAL*　*[TURN*　*DIRECT]*
TION

TRANSFER

Soku　　shō　　mu　　shō　　shin

速　　証　　無　　生　　身

QUICKLY　　*DEMON-*　　*(-LESS)*　　*REINCARNATE*　　*BODY*
　　　　　STRATE

Verse of the Original Vows

Amida Buddha's Original Vows are

> *the principal gate to the (Pure Land of) Ultimate Bliss.*

Through the transference of merits of the practice through mental concentration, and the practice that can be done even when mentally distracted as well,

> *we will (be born in the Pure Land and) quickly attain the body which will never born again.*

Honzeige is an excerpt from the opening verse of the *Commentary on Meditation Sutra* written by Zendo Daishi. The phrase "the practice through mental concentration, and the practice that can be done even when mentally distracted as well" appears therein.

The former 'practice' refers to the thirteen intensive meditation methods of visualizing the Pure Land, Amida Buddha, and Bodhisattvas as taught in the *Meditation Sutra,* and the latter refers to the other practices taught in the same sutra without involving visualization. For example, the latter refers to trainings, such as acquiring the Three Minds, understanding the Mahayana Sutras, adhering to the precepts, being filial to one's parents, being able to chant Junen at the time of one's death despite evil deeds, or the like.

Honzeige teaches that we should transfer these merits of practices for Birth in the Pure Land and quickly liberate ourselves from transmigration of birth-and-death.

Jodo Shu, however, does not say that one cannot attain Birth in the Pure Land unless one performs these practices in addition to Nembutsu. Although these practices are not essential for Birth, Honzeige teaches that if you do them, you should transfer the merits of those practices for Birth in the Pure Land.

Please refer to the commentary on *Ekohotsuganshin* in *Ichimai Kishomon*.

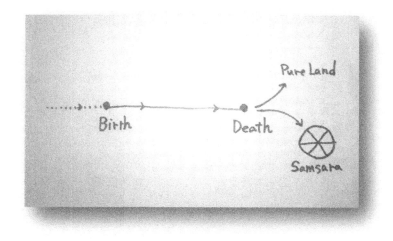

9

Jū nen

十　　念

TEN　　NEMBUTSU

Na mu a mi da bu
南無阿弥陀仏

Na mu a mi da bu
南無阿弥陀仏

Na mu a mi da bu
南無阿弥陀仏

Na mu a mi da bu
南無阿弥陀仏

Na mu a mi da bu
南無阿弥陀仏

Na mu a mi da bu
南無阿弥陀仏

Na mu a mi da bu
南無阿弥陀仏

Na mu a mi da bu
南無阿弥陀仏

Na mu a mi da butsu
南無阿弥陀仏

Na- mu a mi da bu-
南無阿弥陀仏

In the previous section of Junen, I have explained the 18th Original Vow of Amida Buddha (Dharmakara Bodhisattva). Now I would like to introduce a passage from Zendo Daishi's *Commentary on Meditation Sutra*, which is said to be Verse on the Founding of Jodo Shu.

With undivided attention wholeheartedly call on Amida Buddha's Name— whether walking, standing, sitting or lying down—without questioning the length of time. To call Amida's Name steadily is called the "Rightly Established Practice" for it is in accordance with Amida's Original Vow.

Zendo Daishi (613–81) was a high priest in the era of the Tang Dynasty in China. He established the idea of Birth in the Pure Land through Nembutsu, and had a great influence on Japanese Pure Land Buddhism. The above-mentioned **1** Koge, **3** Sanbujo, **6** Raisan, and **9** Honzeige, and **14** Soekoge and **18** Sobutsuge explained later are also quoted from his works.

The text he wrote, the *Commentary on Meditation Sutra*, had a great influence on Honen Shonin, and the verse introduced here, in particular, served as the impetus for Honen Shonin to open Jodo Shu. It is clearly stated there that Amida Buddha's original vow guarantees Birth in the Pure Land. This verse convinced Honen Shonin that there was no need for any other practices, and that just the practice of Nembutsu would lead us to Birth.

10

Shūso Hōnen Shōnin Go-yuikun

宗祖 法然上人 ご遺訓

Ichimaï Kishōmon

一枚起請文

Morokoshi waga chō ni, moromoro no chisha tachi no

唐土　我朝に、　もろもろの　智者達の、

CHINA (ancient name)　*JAPAN* (ancient name)　　*VARIOUS*　　　*WISE MEN*

satashi mōsaruru kan'nen no nen　nimo arazu.

沙汰し申さるる　観念の　念 にもあらず。

ARGUE　　*VISUALIZATION*　*NEN*　　　*NOT*

Mata gakumon wo shite nen no kokoro wo satorite　mōsu

また 学問を　して、念の こころを 悟りて　申す

OR　*STUDY*　*DO*　*NEN*　*HEART*　*UNDERSTAND* *SAY/RECITE*

Nembutsu nimo　arazu.

念仏にも　あらず。

NEMBUTSU　　　*NOT*

Tada　ōjō　gokuraku no　tame niwa,

ただ 往生　極楽の　ためには、

JUST　*GO BE BORN*　*(THE LAND OF) ULTIMATE BLISS*　*FOR THE PURPOSE OF*

Namu Amida Butsu　to　mōshite,

南無阿弥陀仏　と 申して、

NAMU AMIDA BUTSU　*(THAT)*　*RECITE*

utagaï　naku　ōjō　suruzo to　omoi torite

うたがい なく　往生 するぞと 思い取りて

DOUBT　*-LESSLY*　*GO BE BORN*　*DETERMINE*　*FULLY GRASP*

mōsu　hoka niwa　betsu no shisaï　sōrawazu.

申す 外には　別の 仔細 候わず。

RECITE　*OTHER THAN*　*SEPARATE*　*DETAILS*　*NOT PRESENT*

One-sheet Testament

~ *Honen Shonin's parting message* ~

In China and Japan, various Buddhist masters and scholars

have argued that Nen (of Nembutsu) means visualization (of Amida Buddha and the Pure Land). But that's not it.

By studying (Buddhist scriptures and the interpretations of them), you might understand the heart of Nen (of Nembutsu) and after that say

Nembutsu, but neither is that.

For the purpose of going and being born (Birth, Ojo) (in Amida Buddha's) Land of Ultimate Bliss,

it is through the recitation of "Namu Amida Butsu"

that Birth can be doubtlessly attained—You should fully grasp this and

just recite (Nembutsu). Other than that, there is no implication.

Tadashi sanjin shishu to   mōsu   koto no sōrō wa,
ただし 三心四修 と 申す ことの候うは、
HOWEVER   SANJIN SHISHU   (THAT) DISCUSS   THERE ARE CASES

mina ketsujō shite Namu Amida Butsu nite
皆　決定して　南無阿弥陀仏　にて
ALL   RESOLUTELY   NAMU AMIDA BUTSU   THROUGH

ōjō   suruzo to omou uchi ni   komori sōrō nari.
往生　するぞと思う うちに こもり候うなり。
GO BE BORN   DETERMINE   THINK   IN   INCLUDED

Kono hoka ni   oku fukaki koto wo zonzeba,
この　外に　奥深き　事を　存ぜば、
THIS   OTHER THAN   HIDDEN DEEPLY   THING   THINK

nison no   awaremi ni   hazure,
二尊の　あわれみにはずれ、
TWO HONORED ONE'S   COMPASSION   DETACH

hongan ni   more   sōrō beshi.
本願に　もれ　候うべし。
ORIGINAL VOW BE DEVIATED   WILL

Nembutsu wo shinzen hito wa,
念仏を　信ぜん 人は、
NEMBUTSU   BELIEVE   ONE

tatoi ichidaï no hō wo   yokuyoku gakusu tomo,
たとい 一代の　法を　よくよく 学すとも、
EVEN IF   LIFETIME   TEACHINGS   THOROUGHLY   STUDY

ichimon fuchi no gudon no mi ni nashite,
一文　不知の　愚鈍の　身に なして、
ONE LETTER   NOT KNOW   FOOL   SELF   SEE AS

Ama nyūdō no muchi no tomogara ni onajiu shite,
尼　入道の 無智の ともがらに 同じうして、
NUN   MONK   IGNORANT   COMRADE   SAME   SEE AS

However, there are cases where Sanjin and Shishu are discussed,

all of which are included in the resolution

to attain Birth definitely through (the recitation of) "Namu Amida Butsu."

If you think that there is something deeply hidden other than this,

you will not be able to receive the compassion of the two Honored Ones (Sakyamuni and Amida),

and will be deviated from (the salvation of Amida's) Original Vow.

Any of you who believe in Nembutsu,

even if you have thoroughly studied the teachings that Sakyamuni taught during his lifetime,

see yourself as a fool who doesn't even know a single letter, and

see yourself to be the same as ignorant comrades like self-proclaimed nuns or monks (who just shave their heads and know nothing about Buddhism),

chisha no furumaï wo sezu shite
智者の ふるまいを せずして
WISE PERSON ACT WITHOUT DOING

tada ikkō ni Nembutsu subeshi.
ただ一向に 念仏 すべし。
JUST INTENTLY NEMBUTSU SHOULD DO

Shō no tame ni ryōshuïn wo mottesu.
証の ために 両手印を もってす。
PROOF FOR THE PURPOSE OF BOTH HANDS PRINT USE

Jōdo Shū no anjin kigyō kono isshi ni shigoku seri.
浄土宗の 安心 起行 この 一紙に 至極せり。
JODO SHU BELIEF PRACTICE THIS SINGLE SHEET THOROUGHLY SUMMARIZED

Genkū[10] ga shozon, konohoka ni mattaku betsugi wo zonzezu.
源空が 所存、 この外に 全く 別義を 存ぜず。
GENKU'S THOUGHT BESIDES THIS ANY OTHER THING NOT PRESENT

Metsugo no jagi wo fusegan ga tame ni
滅後の 邪義を ふせがんが ために
DEATH AFTER FALSE TEACHING PREVENT FOR THE PURPOSE OF

shozon wo shirushi owannu.
所存を しるし 畢んぬ。
THOUGHT WRITE DOWN COMPLETED

Kenryaku[11] ni nen shōgatsu nijū-san nichi.
建暦 二年 正月 二十三日
KENRYAKU SECOND YEAR JANUARY TWENTY-THIRD DAY

Daïshi zaï gohan
大師 在 御判
DAISHI FOUND HANDS PRINT

---

[10] *Genku* is Honen Shonin's personal name, while *Honen* is his name as a monk.
[11] Japanese Era name (1211 - 1213)

without acting like a wise person,

just intently do the practice of Nembutsu.

I (hereby) press both hands print for proof.

The belief and practice of Jodo Shu are thoroughly summarized in this one sheet.

I, Genku (Honen), have no thought other than this.

To prevent false teachings from appearing after my death,

I have written down my thoughts.

January 23rd, the second year of Kenryaku era (1212),

with (Honen Shonin's) hands print.

On January 23rd of 1212, Honen Shonin wrote *Ichimai Kishomon*, a record of his essential teaching, to his disciple Genchi, and passed away to the Pure Land two days later at the age of eighty. *Ichimai Kishomon* is the most famous writing by Honen Shonin, and is always read aloud in daily services in Japan.

"You should just intently do the practice of Nembutsu without acting like a wise person." All the teachings of Jodo Shu are summarized in this one sentence in *Ichimai Kishomon*.

The title can be resolved as follows:

宗	shu	Sect, school, denomination
祖	so	Founder, ancestor, pioneer
法然	Honen	Honen
上人	shonin	Saint, holy Buddhist monk
ご	go	Prefix for honorific expression
遺訓	yuikun	Teachings left by a deceased person; last instructions
一	ichi	One
枚	mai	Sheet
起請文	kishomon	Religious oath in writing

It is also translated as 'Our founding master Honen Shonin's parting message —The One-Sheet Testament' in "OTSUTOME" book published by Hawaii Council of Jodo Missions, or as 'The One Sheet Document' in "Traversing the Pure Land Path" published by Jodo Shu Press.

As for the term 三心 (*Sanjin*) in p. 60, l. 1, the meaning of which is frequently asked by people, 三 (*san*) means "three," and 心 (*shin/jin*) means "mind" or "heart." 三心 (Three Minds) is preached in *Meditation Sutra*.

64

Meditation Sutra shows the classification into nine categories of Birth in the Pure Land depending on the practitioners' qualities and merits. When Sakyamuni Buddha talked about the highest birth in the highest level, He said, "Those who have the Three Minds will assuredly be born in the Pure Land. What are the three? The first one is the Utterly Sincere Mind, the second is the Profound Mind, and the third is the Mind which Dedicates All Merits toward the Pure Land with the Resolution to Be Born There."

Zendo Daishi taught that the Three Minds were essential not only for the highest Birth in the highest level, but also for all nine kinds of Birth.

He also gave a concrete interpretation of the Three Minds.

The Utterly Sincere Mind: 至誠心 *(Shijoshin)*

Zendo Daishi says that Sakyamuni Buddha urged us to do all the acts with a true mind that is full of sincerity. We should aspire to be born in the Pure Land with the utterly sincere mind. We should not put on the appearance of being wise, good, or diligent in our outward relationships when the mind inside is actually an empty void.

The Profound Mind: 深心 *(Jinshin)*

Zendo Daishi says that the Profound Mind is a deeply believing mind, which believes firstly that we have no power by ourselves to get out of the cycle of birth and death that has been going on from everlasting, and also the mind believes secondly that depending on the power of the Original Vow of Amida Buddha we will surely be able to emancipate ourselves from the transmigration and be born in His Pure Land.

Mind which Dedicates All Merits toward the Pure Land with the Resolution to Be Born There: 回向発願心 *(Ekohotsuganshin)*

We must have accumulated a lot of or some merits in the past and present lives through action, speech and thought. We should dedicate all the merits toward the Pure Land with the resolution to be born there, but we should not dedicate the merits toward other purposes like worldly benefit or another Buddhist goal.

Zendo Daishi advocated Nembutsu with the Three Minds like that.

On the other hand, Honen Shonin also emphasized the Three Minds, but he preached, "If you believe in the Original Vow and chant Nembutsu, the Three

Minds will naturally come to you."

Honen Shonin's teaching differs subtly from Zendo Daishi's. For Honen Shonin, believing in the Original Vow of Amida and chanting Nembutsu are the most important things, and the Three Minds are something that follows them.

Next, regarding 四修 (*Shishu*), 四 (*shi*) means "four," and 修 (*shu*) means "practice." This term refers to four modes of the religious practice advocated by Zendo Daishi in his Hymn in Praise of Birth.

The first is reverence shown to Amida Buddha and bodhisattvas in the Pure Land in the form of prostrations before their images and other similar acts of honor. The second is exclusive practice, which means wholehearted and exclusive recitations and meditation on Amida Buddha alone. The third is uninterrupted practice, especially as regards the recitation of Nembutsu. The fourth is a long-term practice. That is, that one pursues this kind of practice throughout the whole of one's life.

Honen Shonin says that these Four Modes of Practice, like the Three Minds, are also included in the practice of Nembutsu with faith in the Original Vow of Amida.

Before the line of the date at the end of the main text, Honen Shonin says,

"To prevent false teachings from appearing after my death, I have written down my thoughts."

In this way, the purpose of Honen Shonin's writing of *Ichimai Kishomon* is finally explained. Then, what exactly are false teachings that might appear after his death?

The false teachings mentioned at the beginning of *Ichimai Kishomon* are:

✗ 1) Nembutsu is the visualization of Amida Buddha and the Pure Land.

✗ 2) After studying Nembutsu thoroughly through sutras and their commentaries and understanding them, one can recite Nembutsu.

On the other hand, what Honen Shonin says about these are:

1) [*Honen Shonin*]   Nembutsu is not the visualization of Amida Buddha and the Pure Land, but the act of believing in Amida Buddha's Original Vow and chanting "Namu Amida Butsu."

2) [*Honen Shonin*]   There is no need to study further for Nembutsu as long as one understands the Original Vow of Amida Buddha.

In addition to these, the following teachings could be said to be false. The teachings of Honen Shonin, in contrast, are cited below.

✗ 3)   Nembutsu must be practiced together with the threefold discipline which is morality (sila), meditation (dhyana) and wisdom (prajna).

[*Honen Shonin*]   The threefold discipline is a precious teaching that forms the basis of Buddhism, but it is difficult to practice it in this saha world and in this Mappō (degenerate) period. First, you should be born in the Pure Land through the exclusive practice of Nembutsu, and then undergo the discipline to become a buddha there.

✗ 4)   In order to be born in the Pure Land, in addition to Nembutsu, the six paramitas, filial piety, and social activities are essential.

[*Honen Shonin*]   It is good to do good deeds, but it is not a prerequisite for Birth. Only Nembutsu, relying on the Vow of Amida Buddha, is the prerequisite for Birth.

✗ 5)   Since the faith determines Birth, reciting Nembutsu once is sufficient or it may not be necessary at all.

✗ 6)   Birth can only be achieved by repeating Nembutsu many times. You can't attain Birth with just one-time Nembutsu.

[*Honen Shonin*]   Believing that you can be born in the Pure Land with just one-time Nembutsu, you should continue to chant Nembutsu for the rest of your life.

✗ 7)   Even if you usually recite Nembutsu, you cannot attain Birth if you are in a state of confusion at the time of death.

[*Honen Shonin*]   Amida Buddha will surely come and welcome you at the time of your death by your usual Nembutsu.

✗ 8)   At the time of death, you cannot attain Birth without a good dharma friend who guides you by your side.

[*Honen Shonin*]   That is not always necessary. With usual Nembutsu, Amida Buddha will certainly come to welcome you at the time of your death.

✗ 9)   Evil people cannot attain Birth in the Pure Land.

[*Honen Shonin*]   By believing in Amida Buddha's Original Vow and chanting Nembutsu, everyone can be born in the Pure Land regardless of whether s/he is good or evil.

✗ 10)   It is enough to recite Nembutsu in your heart. No vocalization is required.

[*Honen Shonin*]   You can chant it in your heart without saying it out loud, but the basic principle is to say it out loud.

✗ 11)   In addition to Nembutsu, various practices are also essential to attain Birth. They are the three Pure Land Sutras recitation, practice of worship of Amida, praising of Amida and offerings to Amida, etc.

[*Honen Shonin*]   The reciting of the three Pure Land Sutras and the practice of worship of Amida are not essential for Birth, but only to help the practice of Nembutsu.

✗ 12)   Only those who have a special religious experience such as seeing Buddha during training are saved in the Pure Land after death.

[*Honen Shonin*]   If you believe in Amida Buddha's Original Vow and practice Nembutsu, you will definitely be able to see the Buddha at the time of your death and to attain Birth.

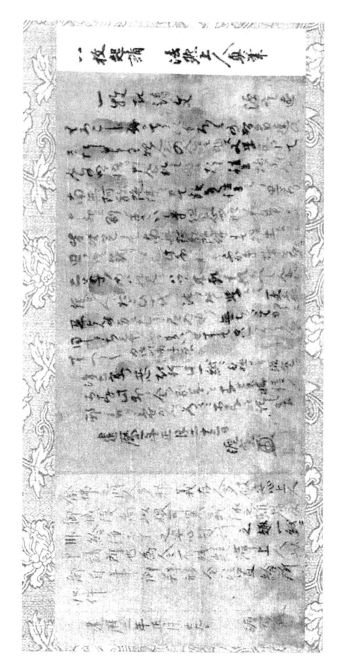

One-sheet Testament – A genuine writing by Honen Shonin

Shō yaku mon
摂 益 文
SAVE   MERIT   VERSE

Kō   myō   hen   jō
光   明   遍   照
LIGHT   BRIGHTNESS   UNIVERSALLY   ILLUMINATE

Ji-   ppō   sé   kaï
十   方   世   界
TEN   DIRECTION   [PERIOD   REALM]
WORLD

Nem   bu-   sshu   jō
念   仏   衆   生
[THOUGHT   BUDDHA]   [PEOPLE   LIFE]
NEMBUTSU   RECITERS

Sé-   sshu   fu   sha
摂   取   不   捨
[SAVE   TAKE]   NOT   ABANDON
SAVE AND RECEIVE

Verse of Receiving (Merit of) Salvation

The essential sentence in Meditation Sutra

Each of these radiant lights universally illuminates

the worlds/realms in the ten directions,

and all the people who recite Nembutsu

shall be saved and received (in the lights of Amida)
and never abandoned.

Shoyakumon is the most important passage in Jodo Shu, though it is a short one which consists of just sixteen (four times four) characters. If we select only one passage to chant besides Nembutsu chanting, this Shoyakumon should be selected.

Shoyakumon is an excerpt from the *Visualization of Immeasurable Life Sutra,* or *Meditation Sutra*. In the sutra, Sakyamuni Buddha preaches to Ananda and Vaidehi about the ways to visualize the Pure Land, Amida Buddha and the two bodhisattvas.

In the ninth visualization Sakyamuni preaches the way to visualize Amida Buddha himself.

Sakyamuni says, "The Buddha of Immeasurable Life has eighty- four thousand major marks and each one of these marks has eighty-four thousand minor marks. Each of these minor marks has eighty- four thousand radiant lights," and

"Each of these radiant lights universally illuminates the worlds/ realms in the ten directions, and all the people who recite Nembutsu shall be saved and received (in the lights of Amida) and never abandoned."

The character 光 (ko) consists of the 火 part and the 儿 part.

The shape of the upper part of the *kanji* originally shows flame and light (火), and the lower part shows human legs (儿), so the *kanji* originally means a halo radiated from someone's head or a torchlight raised overhead.

However, 光 usually doesn't mean a light radiated from someone's head, but just means a light.

The character 明 consists of the 囧 part and the 月 part. It originally shows the moonlight (月) coming through a window (囧).

In Jodo Shu, the word 光明 formed from them denotes the infinite light (immeasurable light) that Amida Buddha is emitting.

Honen Shonin compares the infinite light of Amida to a moonlight in the famous poem *Tsukikage* [月 か げ] (The Moonlight). Probably he did not specifically intend to reflect the origins of these *kanji* in the poem, and such a coincidence is very interesting.

Tsukikage is the official anthem of Jodo Shu now. (You can find its score in the end of this book.)

Tsukikage no itaranu sato wa nakeredomo

月かげの　いたらぬ里は　なけれども
MOONLIGHT   NOT REACH VILLAGE   BE NOT

12

nagamuru hito no kokoro nizo sumu

ながむる人の　心にぞ　すむ
LOOK AT   PEOPLE.   HEART   DWELL

Although the moon shines over
all the villages and villagers equally,

> *the moonlight permeates through only*
> *the hearts of those who stare at it.*
>
> *(Honen Shonin)*

Indeed, Amida's infinite light dwells in the hearts of those reciting His name.

Nembutsu Ichié

念 仏 一 会

NEM BUTSU ONE SERIES

Namu Ami dabu Namu Ami dabu Namu Ami dabu
南無阿弥陀仏 南無阿弥陀仏 南無阿弥陀仏

Namu Ami dabu Namu Ami dabu Namu Ami dabu
南無阿弥陀仏 南無阿弥陀仏 南無阿弥陀仏

Namu Ami dabu Namu Ami dabu Namu Ami dabu
南無阿弥陀仏 南無阿弥陀仏 南無阿弥陀仏

Namu Ami dabu Namu Ami dabu Namu Ami dabu
南無阿弥陀仏 南無阿弥陀仏 南無阿弥陀仏

Namu Ami dabu Namu Ami dabu Namu Ami dabu
南無阿弥陀仏 南無阿弥陀仏 南無阿弥陀仏

Namu Ami dabu
南無阿弥陀仏......

A Series of Nembutsu

The central part of the service

Since the most important practice in Jodo Shu is Nembutsu, Nembutsu Ichie is the central part of Otsutome. Amida Buddha's promise is to save those who call His name into the Pure Land without fail. Please take a moment to chant the Name rhythmically.

Usually the chanting is accompanied by the sound of mokugyo.

The following is a passage from *Amida Sutra*, where Sakyamuni teaches his disciple Śāriputra the coming of Amida to welcome to receive Nembutsu practitioners.

Śāriputra, should good men and good women hear of the teaching of Amida Buddha and assiduously recite the Buddha's name for one day, two, three, four, five, six or seven days, single-heartedly without distraction, then when their lives come to an end, Amida Buddha accompanied by an entourage of sages will appear before them. When their life ends, their minds will not be distracted, and they will immediately achieve Birth in the Pure Land of Ultimate Bliss.

Betsu ékō

別　回　向

SEPARATE　[TURN　DIRECT]
TRANSFER

Special Merit-transference Chanted by the Officiant

Betsu eko refers to a special dedication of the merit we received from chanting of sutra passages and Nembutsu, which is then dedicated to the buddhas, the masters, ancestral souls, and to the protection of our Nembutsu life.

Generally, in Jodo Shu, like other sects of Japanese Buddhism, the merits of performing a memorial service are dedicated for moving forward on the path to enlightenment of the person who passed away by reading the prayer aloud in the service. We chant Soekoge next, and transfer the merit to the Birth in the Pure Land of everyone.

It is traditionally said that you reap what you sow, and Buddhism also basically teaches that you receive the effect of your karma. With the development of Mahayana Buddhism, it was taught that the results of good deeds can be transferred to the benefit of all sentient beings, which began to be gradually emphasized. This background leads to the merit-transference.

There is one more point regarding *eko* that should be mentioned. It is *eko* for your Birth in the Pure Land.

Zendo Daishi preached the Five Right Practices for Birth in the Pure Land. (It is explained in the later Junen section after Soekoge See from p. 82).

Jodo Shu teaches that when you do good deeds other than the Five Right Practices, including Nembutsu, you should transfer the merits for the purpose of Birth in the Pure Land. This is the spirit of Ekohotsuganshin, which is explained as the third of the Three Minds (See p. 65).

Therefore, even outside of Otsutome, it is important to think of your good deeds as being connected to Birth in the Pure Land, rather than doing them for the sake of earthly benefits or other Buddhist purposes.

Thus, it can be said that *eko* in Jodo Shu is not something that is done on one's own effort, but is done based on the power of Amida's Original Vow.

13

Sō ékō gé
総 回 向 偈
WHOLE [TURN DIRECT] VERSE
TRANSFER

Gan ni shi ku doku
願 以 此 功 徳
WISH (BY) THIS DEED VIRTUE

Byō dō se i- ssaï
平 等 施 一 切
EVEN EQUAL GIVE [ONE WHOLE]
EVERYONE

Dō hotsu bo daï shin
同 発 菩 提 心
TOGETHER DEVELOP [BO- DHI HEART]
BODHI CITTA

Ō jō an ra- kkoku
往 生 安 楽 国
[GO BORN] SERENE PEACEFUL LAND
BE BORN

Verse of Merit-transference for All

§ *Dedicating the merits of the service to all* §

We wish these merits and virtues (that we have practiced in today's Otsutome like Nembutsu-chanting, sutra-chanting, seeing the image of Amida and bodhisattvas, flower-offering, incense-offering, etc.)

14

to be equally given to everyone.

And may we together develop bodhi citta (the aspiration for Enlightenment in the Pure Land)

to attain Birth in the Pure Land of Peace and Bliss.

総回向偈 (Soekoge) is a verse of merit-transference for all, in which *eko* means turning the merit and direct/give it to someone.

This is an excerpt from *Commentary on the Meditation Sutra/Visualization of Immeasurable Life Sutra* written by Zendo Daishi.

We don't monopolize the merits of virtue we have practiced in Otsutome, but give the merits to everyone for their Birth in the Pure Land and attainment of Buddhahood in the Pure Land.

This statement is based on bodhisattva spirit, or Mahayana spirit. Therefore, such an attitude is very important.

The core of Otsutome is Nembutsu Ichie, and it may be said that the most important verse is Shoyakumon, and the second important verse is this Soekoge.

In the OTSUTOME book published by Hawaii Council, this Verse of merit-transference for all is translated as follows:

We aspire for these merits and virtues to be equally bestowed upon all. And may we together develop the aspiration for enlightenment to achieve birth in the Pure Land of Peace and Bliss.

Jū　　nen

十　　念

TEN　　NEMBUTSU

Na mu a mi da bu　　　Na mu a mi da bu
南無阿弥陀仏　　　南無阿弥陀仏

Na mu a mi da bu　　　Na mu a mi da bu
南無阿弥陀仏　　　南無阿弥陀仏

Na mu a mi da bu　　　Na mu a mi da bu
南無阿弥陀仏　　　南無阿弥陀仏

Na mu a mi da bu　　　Na mu a mi da bu
南無阿弥陀仏　　　南無阿弥陀仏

Na mu a mi da butsu Na- mu a mi da bu-
南無阿弥陀仏　　　南無阿弥陀仏

The following is the passage from Chapter 16 of *Senchaku Hongan Nembutsu Shu* [選択本願念仏集] (Passages on the Selection of the Nembutsu in the Original Vow). It can be considered the conclusion of Honen Shonin's teachings, which is consistent with the substance of *Ichimai Kishomon*.

Here, Honen Shonin starts his teaching with "There are two superb teachings (to the enlightenment)," and divides all the excellent teachings of Sakyamuni into two. In conclusion, the path we should take is converged into the exclusive practice of Nembutsu.

> *If you hope to depart immediately from the delusive worlds of the transmigration of birth-and-death, you should, within two categories of excellent teachings, put aside the Holy Path and select the Pure Land Path.*
>
> *If you wish to enter the Pure Land Path, of the two practices the Right and the Miscellaneous you should temporarily abandon the various Miscellaneous Practices, and select to take refuge in the Right Practices.*
>
> *In order to pursue the Right Practices, you must choose to devote yourselves to performing the Rightly Established Practice between the Auxiliary Acts and the Rightly Established Practice.*
>
> *The Rightly Established Practice refers to the vocalization of the name of Amida Buddha. Reciting His name guarantees Birth in the Pure Land because it is in accordance with the Original Vow of Amida Buddha.*

In the first paragraph, the Holy Path refers to the cultivation of the threefold discipline (higher virtue, higher mind, higher wisdom) through which the practitioner eliminates his/her defilements and realizes enlightenment by virtue of his/her own efforts, while alive in the present life. Next, the Pure Land Path refers to the practice if relying solely on the compassion of Amida Buddha, through which the practitioner attains Birth in the Pure Land while still laden with his/her defilements, and ultimately realizes enlightenment there.

In the second paragraph, according to Zendo Daishi, the Five Right Practices for Birth in the Pure Land are: (1) reading and reciting the three Pure Land Sutras; (2) visualizing Amida Buddha and the majestic adornments of the Pure Land; (3) prostrating oneself before Amida Buddha; (4) reciting the name of Amida Buddha; and (5) praising Amida Buddha with offerings. The Miscellaneous Practices are all Buddhist practices with the exception of the above Five Right Practices.

In the third paragraph, the Auxiliary Practices are the Five Right Practices with the exception of the (4) of Rightly Established Practice (reciting the name of Amida Buddha).

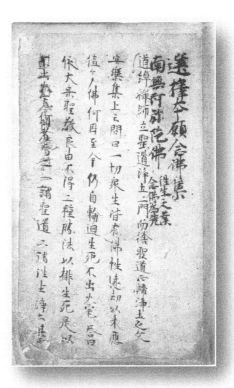

*The opening of the Senchaku
Hongan Nembutsushu*

Sō gan gé
総 願 偈
WHOLE VOW VERSE

Shu	jō	mu	hen	séi	gan	do
衆	生	無	辺	誓	願	度
[PEOPLE	*LIFE]*	*NO*	*LIMIT*	*VOW*	*WISH*	*SAVE*

SENTIENT BEINGS

Bon	nō	mu	hen	séi	gan	dan
煩	悩	無	辺	誓	願	断
[WORRY	*DISTRESS]*	*NO*	*LIMIT*	*VOW*	*WISH*	*RENOUNCE*

WORLDLY DESIRES

Hō	mon	mu	jin	séi	gan	chi
法	門	無	尽	誓	願	知
DHARMA	*GATE*	*(-LESS)*	*EXHAUST*	*VOW*	*WISH*	*KNOW*

Mu	jō	bo	daï	séi	gan	shō
無	上	菩	提	誓	願	証
UN-	*SURPASSED*	*BO-*	*DHI*	*VOW*	*WISH*	*ATTAIN*

Ji	ta	hō	kaï	dō	ri	yaku
自	他	法	界	同	利	益
SELF	*OTHERS*	*DHARMA*	*REALM*	*SHARE*	*[ADVANTAGE*	*MERIT]*

BLESSING

Gu	shō	goku	raku	jō	butsu	dō
共	生	極	楽	成	仏	道
TOGETHER	*BORN*	*[ULTIMATE*	*BLISS]*	*ATTAIN*	*BUDDHA*	*PATH*

SUKHAVATI

Verse for General Vows

ℓ Expressing our vows as a Mahayana Buddhist ʃ

There are countless people, but I vow to save them all (lead them all to enlightenment).

>*There is no limit to worldly desires, but I vow to renounce them all.*

There are inexhaustible teachings of Buddhism, but I vow to know them all.

>*I vow to attain the unsurpassed enlightenment.*

May myself and others in the world share the same blessings,

>*And be born together in the (Pure Land of) Ultimate Bliss to attain the path of the Buddha (enlightenment).*

This verse originates from Genshin [源信]'s Ōjōyōshū [往生要集] (The Essentials of Birth in the Pure Land).

In Tendai Chigi (Zhìyǐ) [天台智顗]'s Makashikan [摩訶止観] (Mahayana Practice of Cessation and Contemplation), there are four lines that are almost the same as the first four lines of Sōgangé, and it is chanted by many sects as '*Shiguseigan (mon)*' [四弘誓願文] (Four Great Vows).

These four lines represent vows common to all Bodhisattvas and Buddhists of Mahayana Buddhism. Specifically, the points of these four vows are: 度 (Do: save), 断 (Dan: renounce), 知 (Chi: know), and 証 (Shō: attain).

While we, followers of Jodo Shu, here confirm and respect the four vows, which are the basis of Mahayana Buddhism, the full-fledged practice and fulfillment of the four vows will come after our Birth in the Pure Land through the practice of Nembutsu.

In the last two lines, we express our determination, "Let's all be born in the Pure Land and become enlightened in that land."

In the OTSUTOME book published by Hawaii Council, this Verse for General Vows is translated as follows:

> *However innumerable sentient beings are,*
> > *I earnestly vow to enlighten them all.*
> *However inexhaustible delusions are,*
> > *I earnestly vow to extinguish them all.*
> *However immeasurable the Buddha's Teachings are,*
> > *I earnestly vow to comprehend them all.*
> *However incomparable enlightenment is,*
> > *I earnestly vow to attain it by all means.*
> *I sincerely wish to share the blessing with all beings,*
> > *Together we are born into the Pure Land of Ultimate Bliss to achieve the way of the Buddha.*

16

San jin raï

三　身　礼

THREE　BODY　BOW

Na	mu	saï	hō	goku	raku	sé	kaï
南	無	西	方	極	楽	世	界
NA-	*MU*	*WEST*	*DIRECTION*	*[ULTIMATE*	*BLISS]*	*[PERIOD*	*REALM]*
					SUKHAVATI		*WORLD*

Hon	gan	jō	ju	shin	a	mi	da	bū
本	願	成	就	身	阿	弥	陀	仏
ORIGINAL	*VOW*	*[ATTAIN*	*ACCOM-PLISH]*	*BODY*	*A-*	*MI-*	*DA*	*BUDDHA*
			ACCOMPLISH					

Na	mu	saï	hō	goku	raku	sé	kaï
南	無	西	方	極	楽	世	界

Kō	myō	sé-	sshu	shin	a	mi	da	bū
光	明	摂	取	身	阿	弥	陀	仏
LIGHT	*BRIGHT-NESS*	*[SAVE*	*TAKE]*	*BODY*	*A-*	*MI-*	*DA*	*BUDDHA*
		SAVE AND RECEIVE						

Na	mu	saï	hō	goku	raku	sé	kaï
南	無	西	方	極	楽	世	界

Raï	kō	in	jō	shin	a	mi	da	bū
来	迎	引	接	身	阿	弥	陀	仏
COME	*RECEIVE*	*[PULL*	*JOIN]*	*BODY*	*A-*	*MI-*	*DA*	*BUDDHA*
		LEAD TO SUKHAVATI						

Bowing to Amida Buddha in Three Virtues

❧ *Worshiping Amida Buddha again* ❦

I take refuge in Amida Buddha in the western World of Ultimate Bliss who,

with His body, accomplished His Original Vows.

I take refuge in Amida Buddha in the western World of Ultimate Bliss who,

with His body, receives us in the Light.

17

I take refuge in Amida Buddha in the western World of Ultimate Bliss who,

with His body, will welcome and lead us there.

The source of this verse is unknown.

We praise the three virtues of Amida Buddha, who is a buddha of sambhogakaya, and offer our devotion and worship to Amida Buddha. The three virtues are:

Amida Buddha attained enlightenment ten kalpa long ago, and fulfilled all the Vows which He made when He was a bodhisattva;

Amida Buddha has emitted the infinite light and received us in the light from the moment he attained Buddhahood to the present, and so will He in the future as well; and

Amida Buddha will surely welcome and lead us to the Pure Land when we leave our bodies.

17

Sō butsu gé

送 仏 偈

SEEING-OFF   BUDDHA   VERSE

Shō	butsu	zui	en	gen	pon	goku
請	仏	随	縁	還	本	国
ASK	*BUDDHA*	*FOLLOW*	*RELATION*	*RETURN*	*ORIGINAL*	*LAND*

Fu	san	kō	ke	shin	sō	butsu
普	散	香	華	心	送	仏
WIDELY	*DISPERSE*	*INCENSE*	*FLOWER*	*HEART*	*SEEING-OFF*	*BUDDHA*

Gan	butsu	ji	shin	yō	go	nen
願	仏	慈	心	遥	護	念
WISH	*BUDDHA*	*COMPASSION*	*HEART*	*FROM-FAR*	*PROTECT*	*CARE*

Dō	shō	sō	kan	jin	shu	raï
同	生	相	勧	尽	須	来
[SIMILARLY	*BORN]*	*MUTUALLY*	*RECOMMEND*	*ALL*	*PLEASE*	*COME*

THOSE WHO WERE BORN

Verse for Seeing off the Buddhas

⟨ Seeing off the Buddhas lastly ⟩

I ask the Buddhas to follow each relation and return to each original land,

Offering incense and flowers, I see the Buddhas off wholeheartedly.

I pray that the Buddhas, with the compassionate heart, will protect us from afar.

1) May those who were already born (in the Pure Land) encourage each other and come all together (to guide me).

2) (I will) be born similarly (in the Pure Land), encourage each other there, and all come back (to save all in this saha world).

18

This is a verse from Zendo Daishi's *Hōjisan*, and is the last verse.

We see off the Buddhas, who have received our repentance, praise, recitation of sutra and Nembutsu, etc., to each land by burning incense and offering flowers.

We pray that They will continue to watch over us even after They return to their homelands.

Traditionally, there are various interpretations of the fourth line.

The third patriarch Ryōchū [良忠] interprets 同生 (*dōshō*) as "persons who have already been born in the Pure Land," and based on this interpretation, the fourth line would be translated as:

May those who were already born (in the Pure Land) encourage each other and come together (to guide me).

On the other hand, the subjects of the first three lines, that is, the subjects of "ask," "offer," "see off," and "pray" are all in the first person. If the subject of the 同生 (*dōshō*) is also in the first person, "同生" can be interpreted here as "I will be born similarly (in the Pure Land)." Then, the last line can be interpreted as a resolution to *Gensō-ekō* [還相回向].

That is, the phrase can be read as:

(I will) be born similarly (in the Pure Land), encourage each other there, and all come back (to save all in this saha world).

This interpretation is also consistent with a phrase in Zendo Daishi's *Hotsuganmon* [発願文], which is:

After my Birth in the Pure Land, I will gain the six divine powers, and return to the worlds of the ten directions to save the suffering sentient beings there.

Thus, I would like to adopt the latter translation here.

In the OTSUTOME book published by Hawaii Council, this Verse for Seeing off the Buddhas is translated as follows:

May we now call upon all the buddhas to return to their lands.
We offer incense and flowers in appreciation to send them off.
We ask for your compassionate guidance and protection.
May those who have gone before us to encourage us to attain Birth in the
Pure Land.

18

Tei Sei Jū nen

低声十念

LOW VOICE   TEN NEMBUTSU

Na mu a mi da bu   Na mu a mi da bu
南無阿弥陀仏　　南無阿弥陀仏

Na mu a mi da bu   Na mu a mi da bu
南無阿弥陀仏　　南無阿弥陀仏

Na mu a mi da bu   Na mu a mi da bu
南無阿弥陀仏　　南無阿弥陀仏

Na mu a mi da bu   Na mu a mi da bu
南無阿弥陀仏　　南無阿弥陀仏

Na mu a mi da butsu   Na- mu a mi da bu-
南無阿弥陀仏　　南無阿弥陀仏

"Teisei" means "in a low voice."

In the end of Otsutome, I will introduce a poem written by Honen Shonin, which shows the ideal attitude of Nembutsu devotees.

While I am in my body,
The merit of Nembutsu is being accumulated,
When I leave my body,
I shall go to the Pure Land.
In any case for me
I have no worries,
Thus, I don't worry about life and death.

The mausoleum of Honen Shonin

19

Author's Note

So far, I have explained Otsutome of Jodo Shu.

Otsutome is the basic content for us priests. As you can see, it contains many precious teachings and is very well constructed. It is no exaggeration to say that it is a "Treasure of Jodo Shu."

However, it may be difficult for people in general who are busy and do not have enough time to chant everything. For those people, I will introduce abridged versions 1 to 5.

The full version of Otsutome has the following structure.

1	Koge	Burning incense to purify our body and mind
2	Sanborai	Worshiping the Three Treasures as a Buddhist
3	Sanbujo	Welcoming the Buddhas to the dojo
4	Sangege	Repenting our evil karmas before the Buddhas
5	Junen	Ten recitations of Nembutsu
6	Raisan	Praising Amida Buddha and the Pure Land with a melody
7	Kaikyoge	Opening verse for sutra chanting
8	Shiseige	Excerpt from *Sutra of Immeasurable Life*
9	Honzeige	Verse of the Original Vows
10	Junen	
11	Ichimai Kishomon	Honen Shonin's parting message
12	Shoyakumon	The essential sentence in *Meditation Sutra*
13	Nembutsu Ichie	The central part of the service
14	Soekoge	Dedicating the merits of the service to all
15	Junen	
16	Sogange	Expressing our vows as a Mahayana Buddhist
17	Sanjinrai	Worshiping Amida Buddha again
18	Sobutsuge	Seeing off the Buddhas lastly
19	Teisei Junen	Low-voice Junen

Abridged version 1

3 Sanbujo

4 Sangege

5 Junen

7 Kaikyoge

8 Shiseige

9 Honzeige

10 Junen

11 Ichimai Kishomon

12 Shoyakumon

13 Nembutsu Ichie

14 Soekoge

15 Junen

18 Sobutsuge

19 Teisei Junen

Abridged version 2

7 Kaikyoge

8 Shiseige

12 Shoyakumon

13 Nembutsu Ichie

14 Soekoge

15 Junen

Abridged version 3

12 Shoyakumon

13 Nembutsu Ichie

14 Soekoge

15 Junen

Abridged version 4

13 Nembutsu Ichie

15 Junen

Abridged version 5

15 Junen

The abridged version 5 is only *Junen*! Anyone can do this once or twice a day. You don't have to read aloud difficult sutras.

In fact, in Jodo Shu, Nembutsu is the supreme practice, and chanting of the sutra is positioned as an auxiliary practice that helps Nembutsu practice.

Based on that, if you like any one of them, please try other abridged versions and the full version.

"You should just intently practice Nembutsu without acting like a wise person."

As stated in *Ichimai Kishomon*, this is the religious conclusion of Honen Shonin and the most important teaching of Jodo Shu.

Rather than being caught up in each and every word in the text of Otsutome, it is important to recite Nembutsu while feeling a connection with the great Amida Buddha, and to perform Otsutome as a practice to help it.

Nembutsu is not training, but a reply from your side to the call of Amida Buddha, "Call my Name."

Since Amida Buddha is always calling you to say, "Call my Name," you should forget about yesterday and recite the Nembutsu with a new feeling of today.

Now, let's chant Nembutsu together today, too.

Namu Amida Butsu!

Appendix

Glossary   *(Order of appearance)*

願 gan

As a verb, 願 *gan* generally means (a) to desire, to wish, to hope, to pray. In Otsutome, its subject is "I" or "we."

Alternatively, it means (b) vow(s) made by bodhisattva. In Jodo Shu, it means the 48 vows made by Dharmakara Bodhisattva. Since Dharmakara fulfilled all the vows and became Amida Buddha, the vows are equivalent to the promises that Amida Buddha will assuredly fulfill. Note that the vows in **16** Sogange, however, are common Mahayana Buddhist vows, and "I" is its subject (indicated as (b′)).

Thus, these meanings of 願 *gan* are used in a mingled way throughout Otsutome, which are summarized in the following table.

1 Koge	願我 (gan ga)	(a)
6 Raisan	本願 (hon gan) 願行 (gan gyo)	(b)
	願仏 (gan butsu) 願共 (gan gu)	(a)
7 Kaikyoge	願解 (gan ge)	(a)
8 Shiseige	超世願 (cho sei gan) 願慧悉成満 (gan ne shitsu jo man) 願我功慧力 (gan ga ku e riki) 斯願若剋果 (shi gan nyak-kok-ka)	(b)
9 Honzeige	本誓願 (hon zei gan)	(b)
14 Soekoge	願以此功徳 (gan ni shi ku doku)	(a)
16 Sogange	誓願度 (sei gan do) 誓願断 (sei gan dan) 誓願知 (sei gan chi) 誓願証 (sei gan sho)	(b′)
17 Sanjinrai	本願成就身 (hon gan jo ju shin)	(b)
18 Sobutsuge	願仏 (gan butsu)	(a)

我 ga

The term 我 *ga* is used to mean 'I' or 'we' in various (grammatical) cases and numbers according to the context, and sometimes related to 願 *gan*.

Whom the first person designates varies from verse to verse, which are listed in the table below.

1 Koge	願我 (gan ga)	my	
4 Sangege	我昔 (ga shaku) 我今 (ga kon)	I	Practitioner
6 Raisan	哀愍覆護我 (ai min fu go ga)	me	
7 Kaikyoge	我今 (ga kon)	I	
8 Shiseige	我建 (ga gon), etc.	I	Dharmakara Bodhisattva

Moreover, the first person is sometimes omitted.

3 Sanbujo	奉請 (bu jo)	I/we	
14 Soekoge	願以此功德 (gan ni shi kudoku)	I/we	Practitioner(s)
16 Sogange	誓願度 (sei gan do)	I/we	

香 ko

The term 香 *ko* (incense) is found in **1** Koge and **18** Sobutsuge. Regarding the setting of the dojo (or Buddhist altar), incense, flowers, and candles are prepared centering on the principal image of Amida Buddha. There are several types of incense, such as burnt incense, incense powder, and incense sticks. Burning soothing incense and ringing an *orin* with a pleasant sound can create an extraordinary atmosphere in a dojo.

It is not recommended to change the type of incense (fragrance) too often because it is important to create a stable environment and induce an undisturbed religious feeling for Otsutome.

心 shin

1 Koge	願我心如 (gan ga shin nyo)
2 Sanborai	一心敬礼 (i-sshin kyo rai)
6 Raisan	至心 (shi shin)
11 Ichimai Kishomon	三心 (sanjin) 安心 (anjin)
14 Soekoge	菩提心 (bodai shin)
18 Sobutsuge	心送仏 (shin so butsu) 慈心 (ji shin)

The shape of the *kanji* "心" is said to come from the heart. The word "心" may refer to either a heart or a mind, although it is sometimes used without regard to the distinction between the two.

In the case of "願我心如智慧火 (in **1** Koge)," the emphasis is rather on the meaning of 'mind.' In Mahayana Buddhism, however, wisdom or understanding preached there is inseparable from a compassionate heart.

戒 kai

Found in **1** Koge. "戒 kai" (śīla, precept) is an ethical code that Buddhists should follow, represented by the following five precepts:

(i)   Abstain from killing,

(ii) Abstain from stealing,

(iii) Abstain from sexual misconduct,

(iv) Abstain from wrong speech, and

(v)   Abstain from the use of intoxicating substances that cause inattention.

In Jodo Shu, keeping precepts is not a requirement for Birth in the Pure Land. The only necessary condition for the Birth is the practice of Nembutsu according to Amida Buddha's Original Vow. However, we should keep the precepts as much as possible, and reflect deeply on the transgressions we have already committed. Refer to **4** Sangege.

定 jo

Found in **1** Koge. 定 *jo* (samādhi) means a meditation practice. In Jodo Shu, there is a word "*Nembutsu Zammai* (Nembutsu Samādhi)" whose meaning is to concentrate on recitation of Nembutsu. However, so-called meditation practices such as zazen, shikan, or visualization are not practiced because they are not consistent with the Original Vow of Amida Buddha.

十方/六方 jippo/roppo

The term 十方 *jippo* means ten directions (that is, all the directions), as with 六方 *roppo* (six directions). See the footnote in **1** Koge.

1 Koge	十方三世仏 (ji-ppo san ze bu)
2 Sanborai	十方法界 (ji-ppo ho kai)
3 Sanbujo	十方如来 (ji-ppo nyo rai)
6 Raisan	照十方 (sho ji-ppo) 六方如来 (ro- ppo nyo rai)
8 Shiseige	名声超十方 (myo sho cho ji-ppo) 威曜朗十方 (i yo ro ji-ppo)
12 Shoyakumon	十方世界 (ji-ppo se kai)

三世　sanze

Found in **1** Koge. Sanze, three periods, represents the past, present and future. It refers to the infinity of time, while *jippo* (ten directions) explained above refers to the infinity of space. The concept of infinity is similar to Amida Buddha's "immeasurable life" and "infinite light."

Mahayana Buddhism shows the infinity and transcendency of Buddhahood to us who live in this life that is, or appears to be, limited in time and space.

The terms 常住 *jo ju* in **2** Sanborai and 無量劫 *mu ryo ko* in **8** Shiseige have the same meaning.

仏　bu, butsu

A Buddha, an awakened person. At the beginning of Buddhism, a saint was also called "buddha" even outside of Buddhism.

As Buddhism became organized as a denomination, the word "buddha" turned to refer only to Sakyamuni Buddha.

As mentioned earlier in **2** Sanborai, in the era of Mahayana Buddhism around AD, more buddhas began to appear in the sutra texts. Amida Buddha is one of them.

The background to the emergence of the teaching of "many Buddhas" is as follows. After the death of Sakyamuni, it was said that there would be a long, long period in the absence of Buddha until the appearance of Maitreya Buddha (5.67 billion years later). On the other hand, there were Buddhists who yearned for salvation by some Buddhas of the time. The ideas of salvation by many Buddhas from many Buddha lands were thus conceived by such people. Trainees who supported Mahayana Buddhism met many Buddhas in their meditation experiences, and actively recorded them as written records, which were gradually spreading at that time. These records are the Mahayana Sutras.

Three of main characteristics of Mahayana Buddhism are:

(i)   preaching the eternal Buddha, as in 三世仏 (*san ze bu*) in **1** Koge, 常住仏 (*jo ju bu*) in **2** Sanborai, etc.;

(ii)   preaching that anyone has the potential to become a buddha, which is generally represented as "一切衆生悉有仏性 (*issai shujo shitsu-u bussho*)" (all beings have the buddha nature), and particularly, in Otsutome, as 令法種増長 (*ryo bo shu zo jo*) in **6** Raisan, and 共生極楽成仏道 (*gu sho goku raku jo butsu do*) in **16** Sogange; and

(iii) emphasizing the bodhisattva spirit, that is, the spirit of altruism, as in 願共諸衆生/往生安楽国 (*gan gu sho shu jo/o jo an rak-koku*) in **6** Raisan, the full text of **8** Shiseige, and **14** Soekoge, and 衆生無辺誓願度 (*shu jo mu hen sei gan do*) in **16** Sogange.

Regarding the bodhisattva spirit, since Jodo Shu places the highest priority on Birth in the Pure Land through the practice of Nembutsu, it does not emphasize the bodhisattva spirit or preach that "the path to Buddhahood is to devote oneself to the practice of bodhisattva." However, Dharmakara Bodhisattva's vow is "If people's salvation is not brought, I will give up even my supreme goal of becoming a Buddha." This is the bodhisattva spirit itself, and the path of Birth through Nembutsu was led from it. Therefore, it can be said that Jodo Shu also has a deep connection with the bodhisattva spirit.

Therefore, being led by Amida Buddha, who has immeasurable life (i), anyone can attain Birth in the Pure Land (ii) to eventually become a buddha, and can wish for the Birth and Buddhahood of others (iii) — in these three points, Jodo Shu can be understood as the "Ultimate Mahayana Pure Land Gate."

The term 仏 *bu, butsu*, in Jodo Shu, generally refers to Amida Buddha who leads us to the Pure Land, Sakyamuni Buddha who preached the teachings of Pure Land, and other Buddhas who proved that the teachings are correct. In addition, from the context of Mahayana Buddhism, it may be said that the term includes such ideal of our attainment of Buddhahood.

三界　　sangai

The term 'sangai' literally means Three Realms ([三界]), which is found in **8** Shiseige. The Three Realms include the realm of desire ([欲界], yoku kai), whose inhabitants have sensuous desire; the realm of form ([色界], shiki kai), whose inhabitants have no sensuous desire but still have attachment to material existence; and the realm of formlessness ([無色界], mu shiki kai), whose inhabitants have no attachment to form but still have attachment to mental functions (perception, mental conceptions and ideas, volition, and consciousness of mind).

All of the Three Realms are worlds of obsession and delusion, while the Pure Land is a world transcending these Realms.

報身　　hojin

Hojin means a reward body, saṃbhogakāya. The term 報身 *hojin* is found nowhere in the text of Otsutome. It is only in **17** Sanjinrai that "body" appears as a word indicating the body of Amida Buddha as follows:

with His body, (Amida) accomplished His Original Vows...
with His body, (Amida) receives us in the Light...
with His body, (Amida) will welcome and lead us there (the Pure Land).

Here, I would like to explain the body of Amida Buddha, that is, the idea of the reward body, saṃbhogakāya.

The following is what Sakyamuni Buddha said when he passed away[12]:

My disciples, my last moment has come, but do not forget that death is only the end of the physical body. The body was born from parents and was nourished by food; just as inevitable are sickness and death.

---

[12] "The Teachings of Buddha," published by Bukkyo Dendo Kyokai (2016), pp. 13–14.

But the true Buddha is not a human body: — it is Enlightenment. A human body must die, but the Wisdom of Enlightenment will exist forever in the truth of the Dharma, and in the practice of the Dharma. He who sees merely my body does not truly see me. Only he who accepts my teaching truly sees me. After my death, the Dharma shall be your teacher. Follow the Dharma and you will be true to me.

It is thus said that even after the death of Sakyamuni Buddha's physical body, the enlightenment, which is the essence of the Buddha, will live on forever and continue to guide us through His teachings and practice of them. From this point came the idea that the dharma body, that is, the eternal and immortal dharma, is the essence of the Buddha. In Mahayana Buddhism, in addition, when a bodhisattva made vows, continued a practice, and became a buddha, the body of the buddha was then called a reward body or saṃbhogakāya because it was obtained as a reward for the achievement of Buddhahood.

Unlike the dharma body (dharmakāya), the reward body (saṃbhogakāya) has a concrete personality and actually saves and guides us. Moreover, unlike Buddha's physical body (nirmāṇakāya), it has an eternal lifespan.

The dharma body, reward body, and physical body are three perspectives to more subtly capture the essence of Buddha, and Honen Shonin follows the teachings of Zendo Daishi and regards Amida Buddha as a reward-body Buddha.

In other words, Amida Buddha is an eternal Buddha who does not have a physical body that gets old, sick, and dies like ours, and nevertheless, as a concrete personality, he had become a buddha after a long training, guides us with His light, and performs a practical function of guiding us to the Pure Land when we die.

Brief Biography of Honen Shonin

Honen Shonin was born in 1133 in what is now Okayama Prefecture in Japan. His childhood name was Seishi-maru. His father was Uruma no Tokikuni who played the role of local police to protect public order, and his mother was from the Hata clan. He lost his father in a night attack when he was nine years old. His father's dying words were: "Don't hate the enemy; instead, become a monk and pray for me and for your own deliverance."

After that, he became an apprentice monk and was later sent to Mt. Hiei to continue his training. Eventually, he came to be praised as a monk of great learning, but he himself was not satisfied and went into seclusion and continued his studies.

At the age of 43, he opened his eyes to salvation by Amida Buddha's Original Vow from the words of Zendo Daishi, and founded Jodo Shu.

Following his father's last words, the two major challenges of Shonin were the conviction in his own enlightenment and the salvation of all beings (which would include the salvation of his deceased father and unlearned mother). Both of these challenges were resolved by encountering the teaching of Nembutsu.

His teachings, which clearly showed the common people's Birth into the Pure Land, were enthusiastically supported by people of the time, regardless of their social statuses.

Although being subjected to several times of religious oppression, he survived the ordeals to continuously lead people to the teaching of Nembutsu. He wrote *Ichimai Kishomon* on January 23rd, 1212, and two days after, passed away toward Jodo.

Tsuki kage, the Anthem of Jodo Shu

月かげ

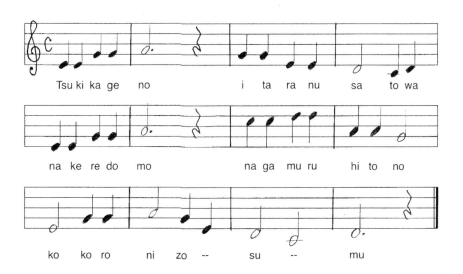

Tsu ki ka ge no   i ta ra nu sa to wa

na ke re do mo   na ga mu ru hi to no

ko ko ro ni zo -- su -- mu

References

English

- "Traversing the Pure Land Path," written by Jonathan Watts and Yoshiharu Tomatsu, Published by Jodo Shu Press (2005).

- "OTSUTOME," compiled by the Otsutome Editorial Committee, published by Hawaii Council of Jodo Missions (2011).

- "The Three Pure Land Sutras," compiled by the Jodo Shu Research Institute, published by Jodo Shu Press (2014).

- "The Teachings of Buddha," published by Bukkyo Dendo Kyokai (2016)

Japanese

- 『浄土宗読誦聖典』高橋弘次, 大谷旭雄監修　四季社 (1998)
- 『日常勤行式の解説』安達俊英著　浄土宗京都教区 (2022)

Acknowledgement

Thank you everyone who has participated in my monthly online service (Live OTSUTOME), and who has asked me various questions. This book largely relies on manuscripts for explaining the sutra verses in Live OTSUTOME, and on answers to your questions.

I would also like to express my deepest gratitude to my wife, Yumiko KASAHARA, who translated each *kanji* in the text into English and designed and edited the entire book.

Special Offer

You can get the original PDF file of this OTSUTOME book from the Rinkaian's website. You can freely edit the file for personal use only.

https://www.rinkaian.jp/downloads/OTSUTOME/

About the Author

Taijun KASAHARA was born in 1958 in Tokyo, Japan. After graduation from Keio University, he worked in the sales and management departments of Nippon Express Co., Ltd. for eight years. As he had taught himself Buddhism until then, he enrolled in Bukkyo University to obtain qualification as a Jodo Shu priest. After working for 10 years at Shinkoin Temple in Tokyo Parish, he launched his new temple Rinkaian in Tama, Tokyo in 2008, where he has been supporting local people, and in addition, in 2014, began providing the teachings in English.

笠原　泰淳

Former Vice-chairman of the Association for the Promotion of Jodo Shu.

Rev. KASAHARA also provides an online monthly service, "Live OTSUTOME." Visit the Rinkaian's website for further information.
https://www.rinkaian.jp/e/

Printed in Great Britain
by Amazon

36315246R00071